BEYOND
the
BLO
MW00995668
Crafty Ol' Broads
a.k.a. Linda K. Johnson
& Jane K. Wells
American Quilter's Society
P. O. Box 3290 • Paducah, KY 42002-3290
www.AmericanQuilter.com

The American Quilter's Society (AQS), located in Paducah, Kentucky, is dedicated to promoting the accomplishments of today's quilters. Through its publications and events, AQS strives to honor today's quiltmakers and their work and to inspire future creativity and innovation in quiltmaking.

Editor: Linda Baxter Lasco
Graphic Design: Lynda Smith
Cover Design: Michael Buckingham
Photography: Charles R. Lynch

Additional copies of this book may be ordered from the American Quilter's Society, PO Box 3290, Paducah, KY 42002-3290, or online at: www.AmericanQuilter.com.

Library of Congress Cataloging-in-Publication Data

Johnson, Linda K.
Beyond the block / by Crafty Ol' Broads aka Linda K. Johnson and Jane K. Wells.
p. cm.
ISBN 978-1-57432-959-9
1. Patchwork--Patterns. 2. Quilting--Patterns. I. Wells, Jane K. II. Title.

TT835.J585565 2008
746.46'041--dc22

2008031185

Proudly printed and bound in the
United States of America

Contents

Skill levels:. . . . .
♥ = confident beginner ♥ ♥ = intermediate ♥ ♥ + = you guessed it, almost advanced ♥ ♥ ♥ = advanced

Introduction

Rewarding, stimulating, frustrating, challenging, joyful, and just plain fun are all attributes of this quilting journey and we love it! We have made wonderful friends, greatly expanded our knowledge, and found immense satisfaction in the design process as well as the actual creation of our quilts. As an added benefit, we have something constructive to think about at night when others are either sleeping or restlessly counting sheep. Our desire is that this book will be a positive contribution to your personal quilting journey.

Beyond the Block is an instructional book of inspiration. This wonderful collection of original and trendy quilts is designed around special motif or theme fabrics. A confident beginner will enjoy the challenges of these patterns, while experienced quilters will be inspired to use this book as a guide to let their creativity shine.

Block placement diagrams are included with each of the quilts, both in the detailed patterns and in the gallery of quilts. Specific instructions for the techniques used in the quilts' construction are arranged alphabetically in the Techniques section (pages 72–93).

We encourage you to use bits and pieces from a combination of the patterns to create your own one-of-a-kind quilt. We'll guide you through the process to fit it all together. The patterns are flexible and fun.

We are extremely thankful for the wonderful friends and students who were willing to test these patterns for us. They patiently offered helpful suggestions while encouraging us with this book.

Testers were instructed to read our directions and use the block placement diagrams as guides but to trade out filler blocks as desired. Some followed the patterns exactly while others made multiple changes before sewing the first stitch. This is yet another joy of the quilting game. How great it is to share in the excitement of our friends' successes!

Thank you for trying our patterns. We so enjoy the designing, piecing, and quilting process and would love to see your finished project.

Please visit our Crafty Ol' Broads Web site at www.craftyolbroads.com or contact us by e-mail:

Jane: wellswildnwooly@aol.com
Linda: lindajohnson07@verizon.net

A Few Thoughts from the Crafty Ol' Broads on the Basics

We both like to design quilts "as we go." We often have an idea, start pulling fabrics (as in many, many fabrics, usually at least four times what we can use), make a couple blocks, put them up on the design wall, and keep working from there. We think that by working spontaneously, the creative juices start flowing and our brains begin to think more freely.

Many of our testers enjoyed working in an organized way, following our patterns and completing one section of their quilt before continuing on to the next. Others started with the focus blocks, then made decisions about additional fabrics and fillers. With our patterns, you can make blocks and fillers in whatever way best suits you and your quilt. Eventually, it becomes easy to make a quilt from a block placement guide without actually reading the instructions.

You will find there are some small discrepancies between the quilt instructions and sample quilts pictured. One of the beauties of this system is that it is easy to add or subtract fillers so that all blocks fit perfectly. We hope that as you try some of our patterns and ideas, you find great joy in creating your own masterpieces.

Our Favorite Tool

A design wall is the one quilting tool we absolutely MUST have. Both of us use a sheet of insulation board, covered with batting and glued or bolted to a wall.

Madison and Garrett Wells often enjoy using scraps to design their own quilts at the bottom of Grandma Jane's much used design wall. Polyester or poly/cotton batting will hold pieces of fabric in place. Larger sections may be pinned in place. Sometimes we view our works in progress from outside, looking through a window, in order to get a different perspective.

Make your design wall as large as space will allow. If you need to put your design wall away, you can cut the insulation board in half and fold it for storage under a bed. Of course, this design wall should not have been glued or bolted to your wall!

BIG, BOLD, AND BEAUTIFUL detail

with an animal print for AT THE ZOO (page 67) and actually planned the quilt around that particular fabric. However, as we worked on the design wall, the fabric just didn't play well with our blocks so very little of it ended up on the quilt top. Still, it was the inspiration for the color scheme.

Color placement can add so much to a quilt's appeal. Note the dimensional zigzag created by the color value of the plaids used in FRIENDSHIP GARDENS (shown below). FRONT YARD GARDENS (page 54) gives a hint of this but the former really showcases dimension. By placing similar values next to each other, as in the big sky background of I GIVE YOU THE SUN, THE MOON, AND THE STARS (page 30), you can create a magnificent backdrop for all the other blocks. A feeling of depth is created with the use of a variety of fabrics in the same color family.

Selecting Fabrics and Colors

Picking fabrics and colors can be the most rewarding as well as the most frustrating part of the quilting process. Our suggestion is to go with a theme, pull focus fabrics, and then use colors found in those fabrics as a guide for your color scheme. We don't make quilts using just one design line because we feel the resulting quilts would lack depth as well as any element of surprise. It is our desire to create art quilts that are fun to look at from a distance as well as enticing enough to be examined and admired up close and personal.

There are many wonderful books that go into detail about the color wheel and complementary colors, so you may want to peruse those for more ideas if you have not yet developed color confidence. Don't worry. The more you work with color, the easier it is to decide what best gives the result you desire.

After you have picked your main fabrics, either make a couple of focus blocks and put them on your design wall or just pin the fabric to the wall. Sometimes the fabric you choose doesn't quite work out as planned. We fell in love

Luminosity is one of our favorite effects. By using warm and cool colors as well as clear and toned colors, Big, Bold, and Beautiful (page 18) simply vibrates. Note that the iris themselves are luminous. In Guatemala en Rojo (page 36) the soft pink batik appliqué background shines when used with the deep bold colors surrounding it.

Clear and toned blues in medium to dark values contribute to a feeling of luminosity as well as depth in Under the Sea (page 24). African Rhythm (page 64) showcases the use of ombre fabric, creating an illusion of luminosity in the upper left corner. Note how that effect was enhanced by the little red squares radiating out from the star. This all adds to a feeling of movement. Using ombre fabric in or around the Flying Geese of Guatemala en Rojo (page 36), That's so Kyla (page 68), and Summer (page 42) also creates movement.

Another way to add interest to your quilts is with the use of the unexpected. Note the unique combination of fabrics in That's So Kyla (page 68). You can't help but wonder about the person who chose them. Throwing in an unexpected color, as was done here with the greens, creates even more interest.

Scale is another consideration when selecting fabrics. Most of our quilts use small-, medium-, and large-scale prints. Don't you think this helps create a sense of drama? Keep an open mind and an open eye as you discover exciting elements in art and nature that you can incorporate into your quilts.

Construction Techniques

Each pattern begins with a list of the techniques used in the quilt's construction, along with the pages where detailed instructions can be found. You'll find specific measurements given in each pattern and general instructions in the Techniques section at the back of the book.

Block Placement Diagrams

Please read the directions and check the block placement diagram when doing your quilt construction. *Note: Both the block placement diagrams and the piecing instructions have the cut measurements!*

We find it useful to put a check mark on the block placement diagram as each component is completed.

Using Focus Fabrics

When cutting your focus fabric for your quilt blocks, you may find that your fabric is better suited for a different size from that specified in the pattern. You can adjust your filler strips accordingly to accommodate the differences in your focus fabric. Place a square ruler over the design to determine what size square or rectangle will best show off your focus fabric motifs.

Likewise, the colors indicated for the strips and fillers should be replaced with colors that complement your focus fabrics.

Large rulers placed over quilt for squaring up.

Starch and Press

We like to use spray starch to give the fabrics body and make them easier to work with. Spray the fabric lightly and press with a hot iron.

Squaring Up Your Quilt

Sometimes you'll trim as you go along, squaring up each section as you progress. Other times it is advantageous to wait until sections are connected or even until after the quilting is complete. See the detailed instructions on page 89.

Pin Basting

Our instructions are for preparing for machine quilting. Proper pin basting greatly increases the chances of a flat quilt that hangs nicely. We like to pin baste on a table or, if the quilt is very large, we will place tables of the same height next to each other.

The bottom layer of your quilt (backing) should be at least four inches larger than the top on all sides. It must be pressed and then firmly held in place on the table, wrong side up. By using large binder clips found in office supply stores, we are able to do this quite successfully. When using clips is not possible, we use painter's masking tape to hold the backing on all sides, taking care to keep it straight and taut.

The batting should be at least two inches larger than the top on all sides. Smooth the batting over the backing, then spread the finished and pressed top over the batting. Starting in the center and working towards the edges, pin the three layers together with 1" safety pins every 2"–3". Pins can be more widely spaced on smaller, lightweight quilts.

Machine Quilting

Books on machine quilting have proved helpful to us, and we recommend that you check some out. One tip for success from us is to "stitch in the ditch" in a few strategic places to secure the quilt before doing free-motion quilting. Always take just a few pins out at a time around the immediate area to be quilted.

Hanging Sleeve

A 4" finished hanging sleeve allows the quilt to hang flat without a bulge; this size is also required if you want to enter your quilt in some judged shows. We always attach our sleeve before we sew the binding on.

Cut the sleeve fabric 8½" wide and as long as the finished width of your quilt. Hem both ends, which will make it slightly shorter than your quilt top. Fold the fabric in half lengthwise, wrong sides together, and pin the raw edges to the top back of your quilt, just slightly below the quilt's trimmed edge. It will be sewn on when you attach the binding to the quilt. The bottom folded edge is then hand sewn with an invisible slip-stitch.

Let it Snow
designed and
made by
Linda K. Johnson
Monroeville, IN
August 2005

Binding

We prefer to use a single-fold binding cut 1¼" wide for our quilts in order to get a flat edge with sharp, mitered corners. With this method, we usually are awarded 100 percent of the points possible for binding in quilt contests. Sewing on the binding secures the top edge of your hanging sleeve.

Blocking

We both love the softly puckered look quilts acquire after they have been washed and dried. Also, when you dampen fabric, the fibers relax enough to be coaxed into shape; then when it dries, the quilt retains that shape. So if you've accidentally distorted your quilt top or quilt block during quilting or pressing, you can square it up by throwing it in the washer or by dampening it with a mist of water.

If you use a washer, you may want to partially dry your quilt in a dryer, then place it on a clean (as in dog- and cat-hairless) carpet. Gently nudge it into shape (use your rulers again) and pin it to the carpet to dry completely. We must confess that we don't have a carpet that clean, so we place a clean sheet on top of the carpet, under the quilt. Voila! A perfectly shaped quilt emerges!

Labels

Don't forget to add a label on the quilt back with your name, the quilt's name, where and when it was made, and any other information you would like to share. We always make our labels on fabric separate from the quilt, then sew them on by hand after the quilt has been quilted. You can use quilt block borders or appliqué to enhance your labels or use a decorative stitch around the edge before attaching it to your quilt.

The Patterns

Detail of AFRICAN SAFARI by Jane K. Wells

Here a Chick, There A Chick, Everywhere a Chick, Chick

32½" x 30", pieced and quilted by Linda K. Johnson

In this happy little wallhanging, we were inspired by the delightful chicken fabric and the fact that we especially love black-and-white with clear colors. For the supporting blocks, we chose mostly tints of the primary colors and relied heavily on small-scale prints and prints that read like a solid. Notice how the two large-scale prints, sunflowers, and white/black flowers add interest. White is used sparingly for sparkle.

Techniques

Bias Vines (page 72)
Borders (page 72)
Checkerboard (page 73)
Fused Appliqué (page 78)
Half-Square Triangles from Strips (page 79)
Log Cabin (page 81)
Paper Piecing (page 84)
Rocking Squares (page 86)
Squares-on-Point Strip (page 88)
Yo-Yos (page 92)

Fabric Requirements & Supplies

¼ yard focus fabric or enough to get at least 3 full motifs for the Rocking Squares
⅛ yard or less of 5 different reds, 3 yellows, 2 greens, 2 blues, 2 whites, 2 large-scale flower prints for strips for blocks and fillers; ¼ yard each of 2 black-and-white prints; and ¼ yard of solid black
¼ yard of 3 different border fabrics
1¼ yards for backing and hanging sleeve
Batting 36" x 34"
Fusible webbing, such as Lite Steam-A-Seam®, 8" x 11"
8–12 buttons for flowers
Binding ¼ yard

Construction Notes

The quilt is assembled in 4 sections (A, B, C, and D) that are then sewn together. As you make each component, place it on a design wall in its approximate position while you're making the next. Use the block placement diagrams as a guide.

Remember that you can rearrange or trade out components and fillers any way you want!

Focus Fabric Rocking Squares

Cut a square 6" x 6" (block 1) and 2 rectangles 4" x 6" (blocks 2 & 3) of focus fabric. If your focus fabric motifs are smaller than the center sizes specified, as was the case in the sample quilt, add a narrow border or two and trim to the sizes indicated.

Add a Rocking Squares border. Trim block 1 to 8" square and blocks 2 & 3 to 7½" square.

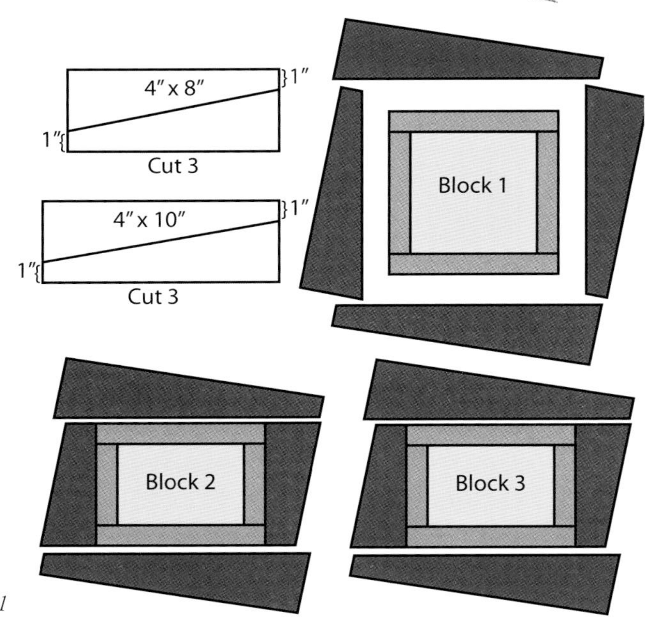

Fig. 1

Section A

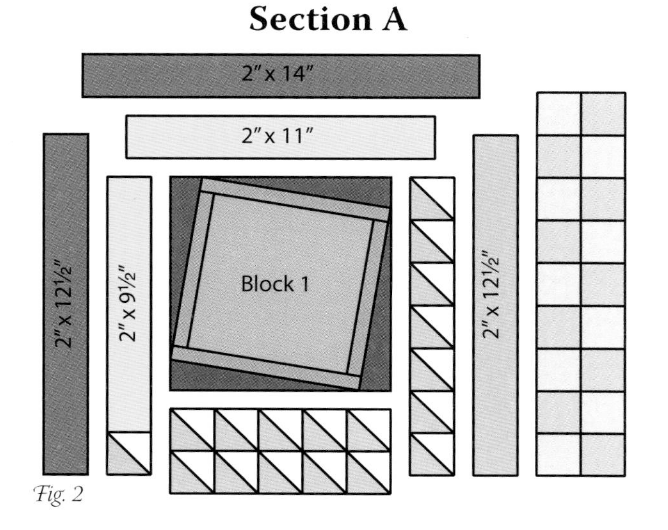

Fig. 2

Half-Square Triangles from Strips

Make 18 half-square triangles from 2½" x 22½" strips. Trim to 2" square. Join with each other and to the filler strips as shown.

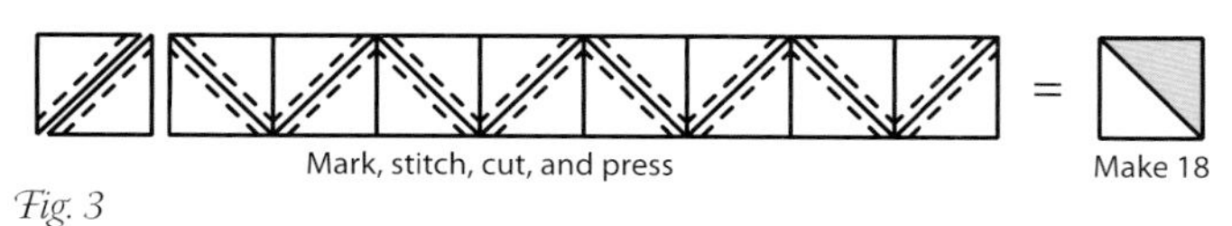

Fig. 3

Sew to block 1 with additional filler strips as shown.

Checkerboard

Make a 9-segment checkerboard from 2" x 18" strips.

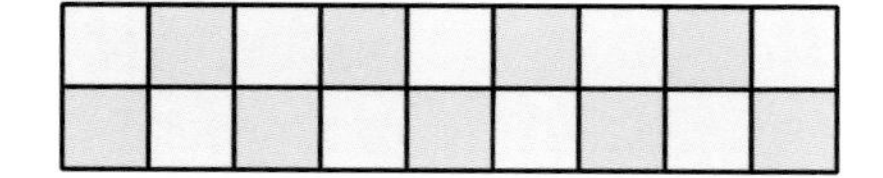

Fig. 4

Add to the block 1 unit to complete section A.

Section B

Filler Strips for Block 2

Cut and add filler strips to block 2 according to the Log Cabin instructions. Trim to measure 12" square.

Add a 5½" x 12" appliqué background.

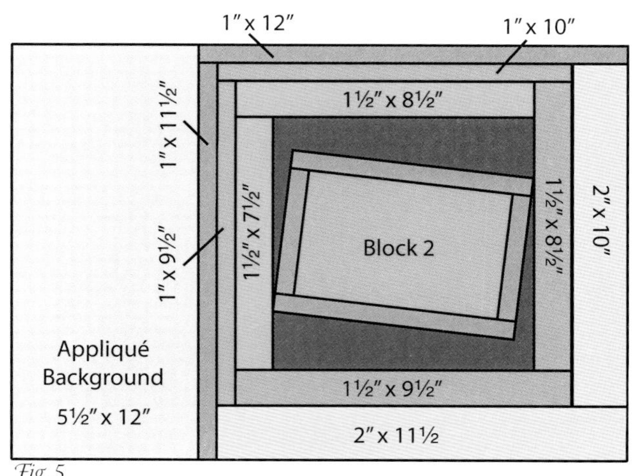

Fig. 5

Fused Appliqué

Make a ¼" bias stem with a 1¼" x 16" bias strip of green. Pin in place in a pleasing curve on the appliqué background, with both ends extending off the edges. Press to ease the fullness and topstitch in place, stopping 1" from the edges of the background. See the sample quilt photo (page 12) for placement.

Trace and cut 4 leaves (page 17). Fuse the lower 2 leaves in place. Set aside the other two.

Cut out focus fabric motifs and add to the appliqué as desired.

Flowers

Make 3 yo-yos with fabric circles 4" in diameter.

Press the yo-yos flat and sew 2 or 3 stacked buttons to the centers, covering the gathering stitches. Set aside to sew on after the quilt is complete.

Section C

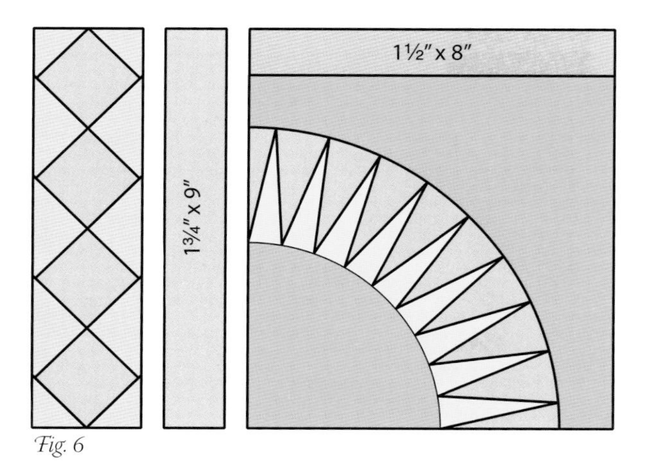

Fig. 6

Sun Block

Enlarge the Sun block pattern on page 17 200%. Trace the center and background pieces onto freezer paper. Cut out the templates.

Press the center and background templates onto two different yellow print fabrics. Cut them out on the cutting line.

Paper piece the Sun ray section and join with the background and center sections. Remove the paper.

Cut and add filler strips to the Sun block as shown

Squares-on-Point Strips

Cut 4 center squares 2" x 2". Cut 3 outer fabric squares 3½" x 3½" twice on the diagonal. Make a squares-on-point unit. Trim to 2¾" x 9". Add to the left side of the Sun block to complete section C.

Section D

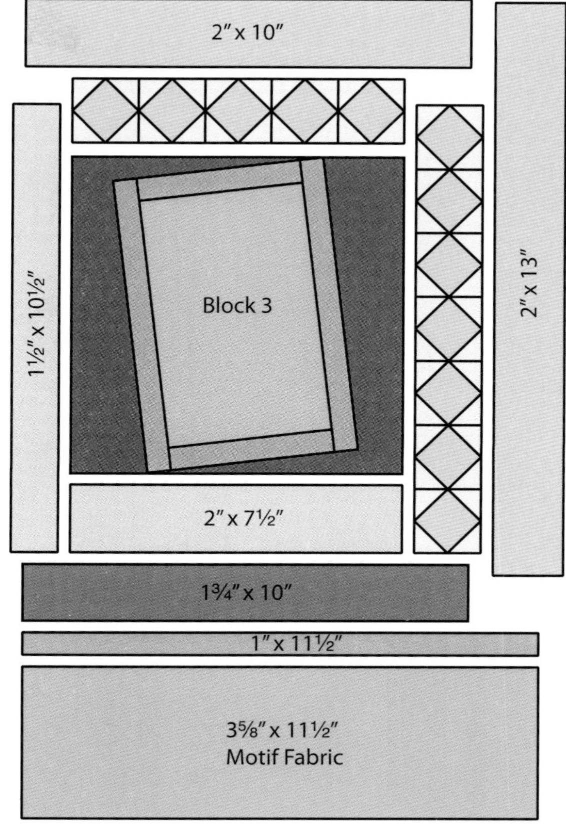

Fig. 7

Fillers for Block 3

Cut 12 center squares 1½" x 1½". Cut 7 outer fabric squares 3" x 3" twice on the diagonal. Make 2 squares-on-point units as shown.

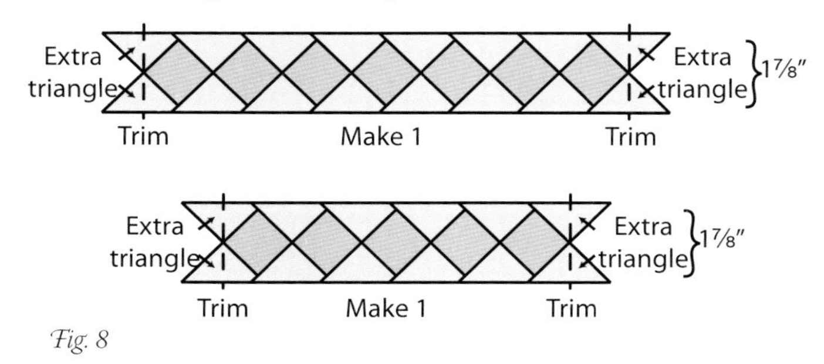

Fig. 8

Cut and add filler strips and the squares-on-point units to block 3 to complete section D.

Finishing

Join the sections as shown.

Pin the loose ends of the appliquéd vine out of the way before adding the borders.

Add a border of 1" wide strips, a second border of 1" wide strips, and a third border of 2" wide strips.

Finish appliquéing the vine in place. Fuse the remaining two leaves in place.

Cut motifs from your focus fabric and fuse in place if desired. See the additional chickens in the sample quilt photo for placement ideas.

Layer the quilt top with batting and backing and quilt as desired. Trim the excess backing and batting. Bind with single-fold 1¼" strips. Sew the yo-yos to the appliquéd stem and finish the stem end with a button.

That's all there is to it!

Fig. 9

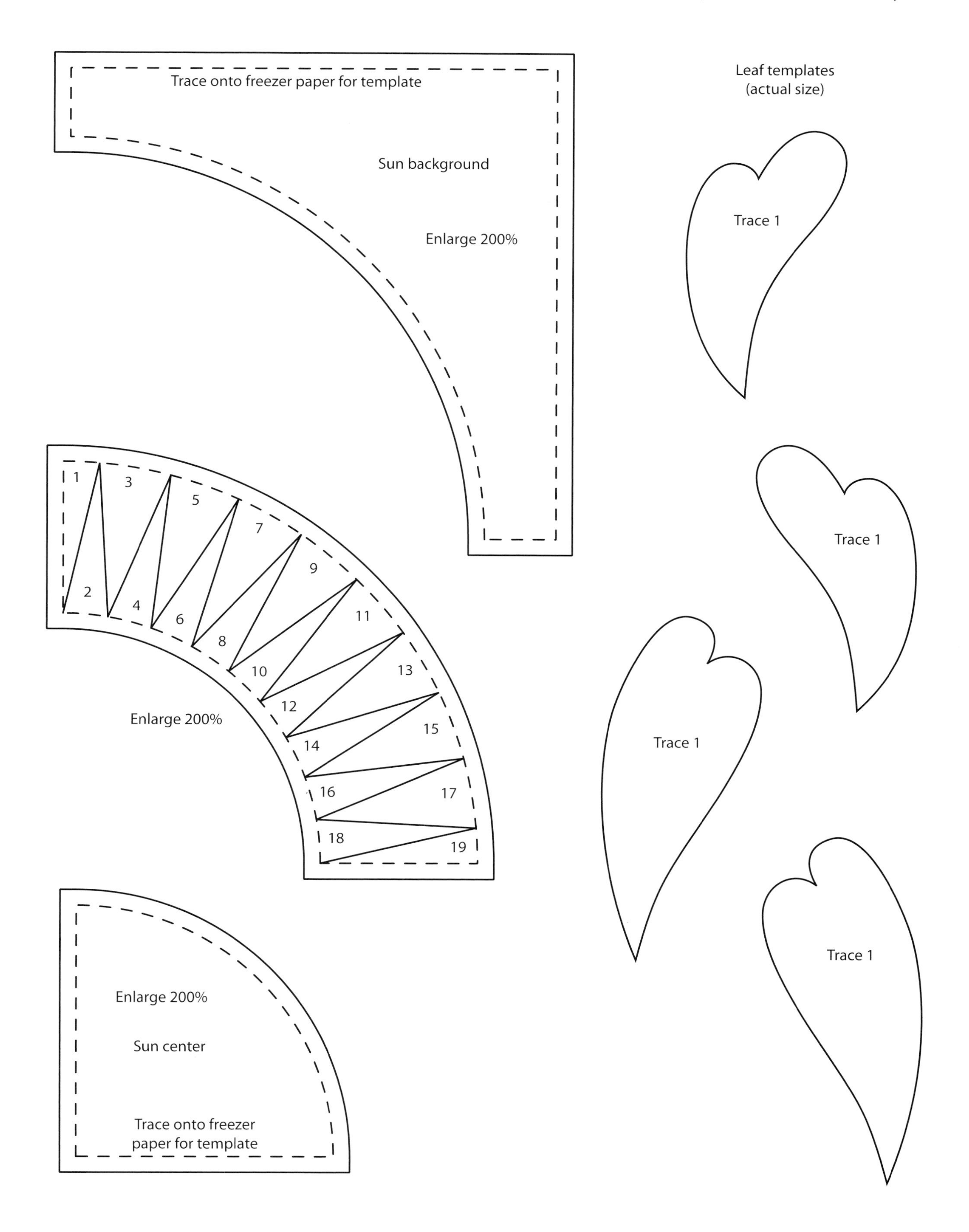
Trace onto freezer paper for template
Sun background
Enlarge 200%
Leaf templates
(actual size)
Trace 1
Trace 1
Trace 1
Trace 1
1
2
3
4
5
6
7
8
9
10
11
12
13
14
15
16
17
18
19
Enlarge 200%
Enlarge 200%
Sun center
Trace onto freezer
paper for template

Big, Bold, and Beautiful

43" x 46½", pieced and quilted by Linda K. Johnson

Here is a beautiful wallhanging quilt that is simple to make, yet simply stunning. Pick a bold focus fabric, surround it with several different blocks of various sizes, then add filler strips to make everything fit together beautifully; hence the name, BIG, BOLD AND BEAUTIFUL (the quilt, not us).

Techniques

Checkerboard (page 73)
Four-Patch (page 77)
Fused Appliqué (page 78)
Half-Square Triangles (page 79)
Nine-Patch (page 84)
Square-in-a-Square (page 88)
Strip Piecing (page 91)
Zipper (page 93)

Fabric Requirements & Supplies

½ yard for setting triangles and a few background filler strips
¼ yard each of 3–7 different theme-related fabrics
¼ yard each of 4 values of the same color for the background fabrics
Scraps from 6 accent fabrics (zingers)
1⅜ yards for the backing and hanging sleeve
¼ yard for the binding
Batting 36" x 48"
½ yard fusible webbing

Construction Notes

The quilt is assembled in 4 sections (A, B, C, and D) that are then sewn together. As you make each component, place it on a design wall in its approximate position while you're making the next. Use the block placement diagrams as a guide.

Remember that you can rearrange or trade out components and fillers any way you want!

Section A

Nine-Patch Units

Cut 2" wide strips from a variety of contrasting fabrics and make 6 Nine-Patch blocks. Refer to the photo of the sample quilt for color placement ideas. (One of these blocks is positioned under and hidden by the appliquéd fish.)

Make a 3 Nine-Patch block unit, a 2 Nine-Patch block unit with a filler strip, and a single Nine-Patch block as shown.

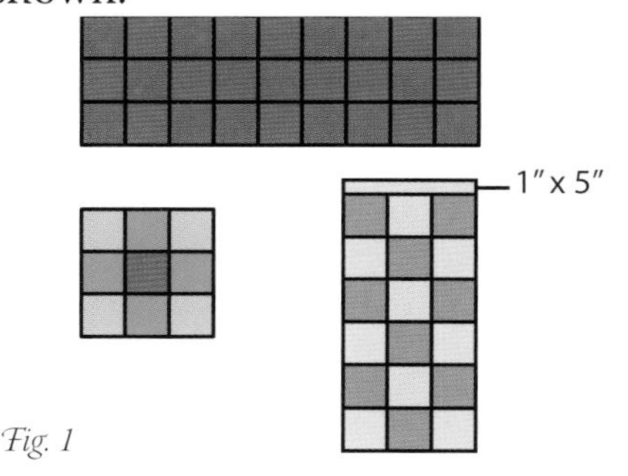

Fig. 1

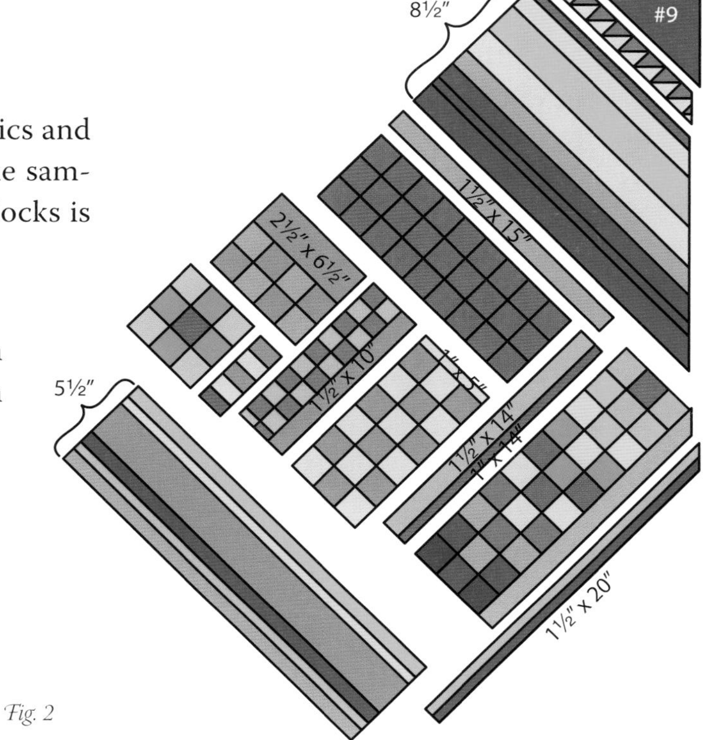

Fig. 2

Checkerboards

Cut 2 strips 1½" x 4" from blue and light blue fabrics and cut into 2" segments. Make a 4-segment, end-to-end checkerboard. Add a 1½" x 2" purple filler strip to one end, as in figure 2.

Cut 2 strips 2" x 8" and make a 4-segment checkerboard, (blue and grey in fig. 2). Add a 2½" x 6½" filler strip to one side.

Cut 2 strips 1½" x 15" of blue and orange fabric and make a 10-segment checkerboard. Add a 1½" x 10" filler strip to one side and trim off the extra checks as shown in figure 2. Join these units with the nine-patch units and filler strips.

Chevron Square Strips

Cut 1 strip 2" x 13" from each of 10 different fabrics including four values of background fabric. Make a strip-set, arranging the fabrics in color/value order. Press the seam allowances all in the same direction.

Cut 6 segments 2" wide. Re-press the seam allowances of two strips in the opposite direction. Arrange the 6 segments in two groups as shown, with the re-pressed strips in the middle.

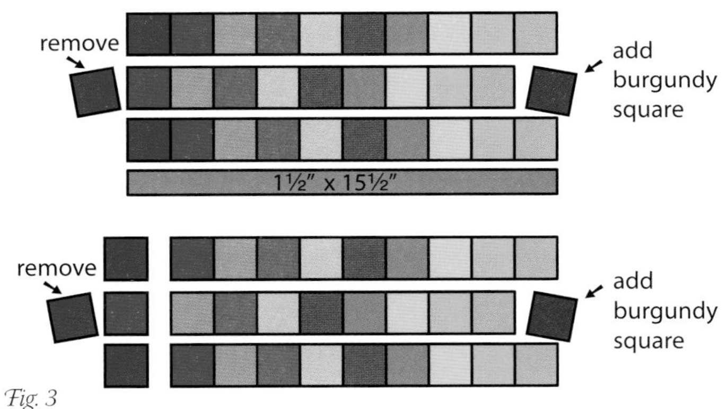

Fig. 3

In the first group, remove the protruding 2" square from the end of the middle strip and sew it to the other end of the same strip, or add a different color square as shown in the example quilt. Sew the strips together. Add a 1½" x 15½" filler strip to one side.

In the second group, remove the protruding 2" square from the end of the middle strip and sew it to the other end of the same strip or add a different colored square. Remove a 2" square from the dark end of each strip. Sew the strips together and set aside for section B.

Add the first chevron square strip to the nine-patch/checkerboard unit as shown in figure 2.

Filler Strip-Sets

Make a strip-set with a variety of 22" strips of focus and zinger fabrics. Trim to 5½" x 21" and add to the nine-patch/checkerboard/chevron square unit.

Make a second strip-set with a variety of 22" strips. Trim to 8½" x 21". Add to the opposite side of the same unit. Add long filler strips as shown in figure 2.

Half-Square Triangles

Make 10 half-square triangles with 2" x 10" strips of contrasting fabric. Trim to 1¾" square and join in a strip.

Add to the 8½" x 21" strip set and roughly trim the strip set at a 45-degree angle. You'll trim it precisely when you square up your quilt.

Setting Triangles for All Sections

Cut 4 squares as shown for the corner and side setting triangles.

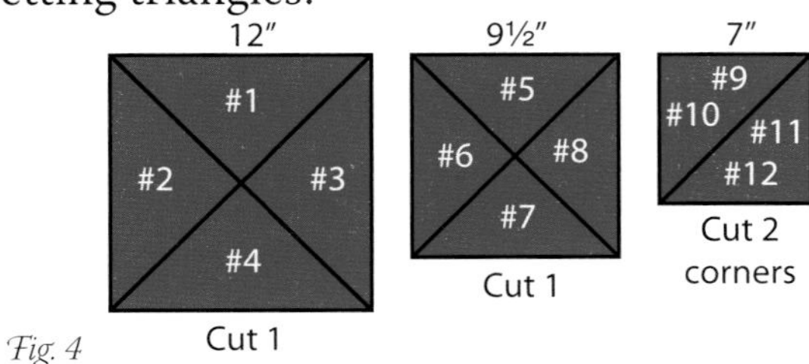

Fig. 4

Pin corner triangle #9 in place to complete section A. Its position is approximate until the other sections are added and you're ready to square up your quilt.

Label and place the remaining triangles on your design wall in the sections indicated in their approximate locations. (See the block placement diagram on page 29.)

Place section A on your design wall and stand back to admire your work of art!

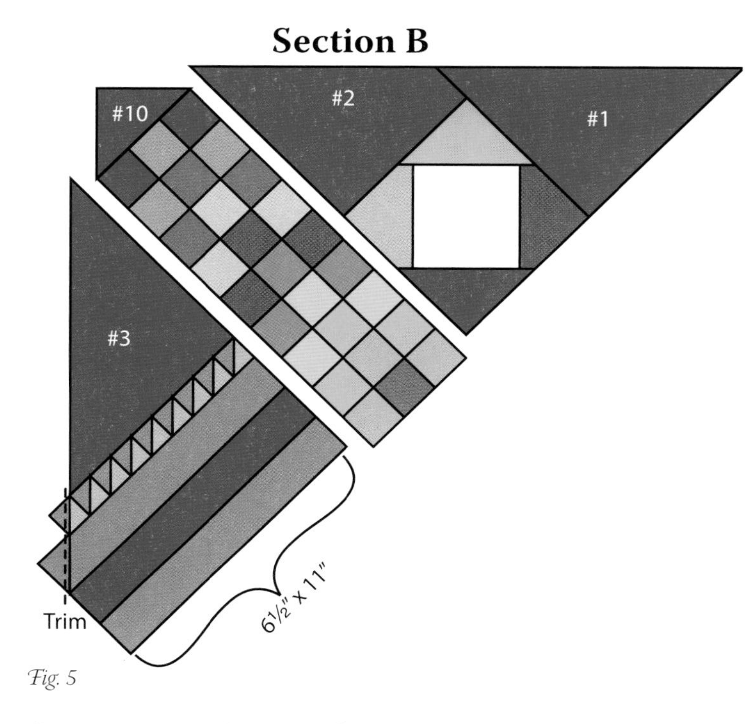

Fig. 5

Square-in-a-Square for Sections B, C, and D

Cut squares as shown and make 5 square-in-a-square units. Set aside a 6½" square-in-a-square for section C and the three 4½" units for section D.

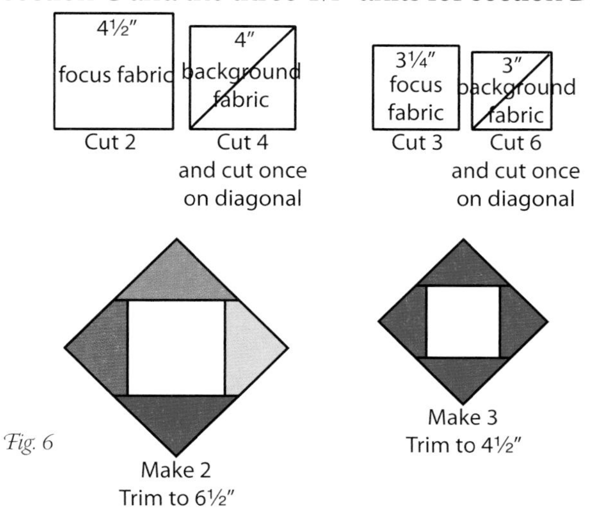

Fig. 6

Variation: Cut some of the background squares from strip-sets.

Add side setting triangles #1 and #2 to a 6½" square-in-a-square, trimming the first triangle even with the edge of the block as shown in figure 5.

Half-Square Triangles

Make 9 half-square triangles with 2" x 10" strips of contrasting fabric. Trim to measure 1½" square and join in a strip.

Filler Strips

Make a strip-set of filler strips, trimming it to 6½" x 11". Add the strip of half-square triangles and side setting triangle #3, aligning the edges as shown in figure 5.

Add corner setting triangle #10 to the 9-segment chevron square strip and join these 3 units to complete section B.

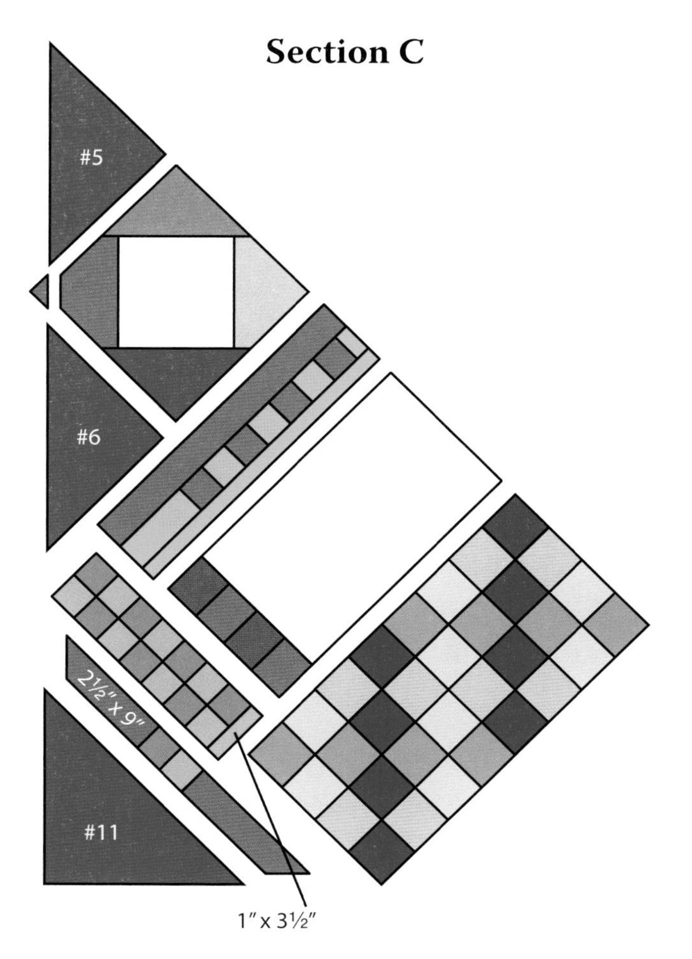

Fig. 7

Square-in-a-Square

Add side setting triangles #5 and #6 to the remaining 6½" square-in-a-square, aligning the triangle edges with the block as shown. Trim the outer tip of the square-in-a-square block.

Zipper

Cut 2 strips 1½" x 6" from contrasting fabric. Make a 4-segment set of zipper "teeth" and add a filler rectangle at the end as shown.

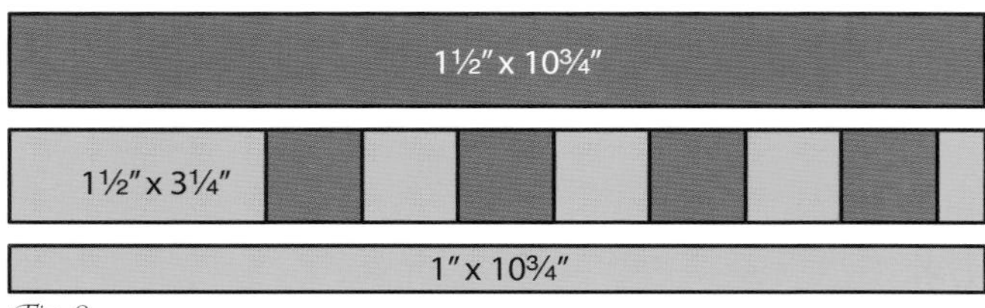

Fig. 8

Cut the outer strips as shown and sew to the sides.

Focus Fabric Block

Cut a 5¼" x 9" rectangle of focus fabric.

Cut 4 rectangles 1¾" x 2" of coordinating fabrics and sew in a row, joining the long edges. Add to the focus fabric block as shown in figure 7.

Join with the zipper unit, trimming it to the same length as the focus fabric block unit.

Checkerboard

Make a 7-segment checkerboard with 2 strips 1½" x 12" of contrasting fabric. Add a filler strip at one end and join with the focus fabric block unit as shown in figure 7.

Four-Patch

Cut 1 strip 2" x 16" from 4 different blue fabrics and make 8 four-patch units. Sew the four-patch units together in a 2 x 4 arrangement and add to the focus fabric block unit as shown in figure 7.

Filler Strip

Add the square-in-a-square unit to the focus fabric unit. Randomly piece a filler strip, or cut a single strip 2½" x 9" and add as shown in figure 7. Sew corner triangle #11 in place to complete section C.

You are three-quarters of the way done. A work of art is emerging!

Section D

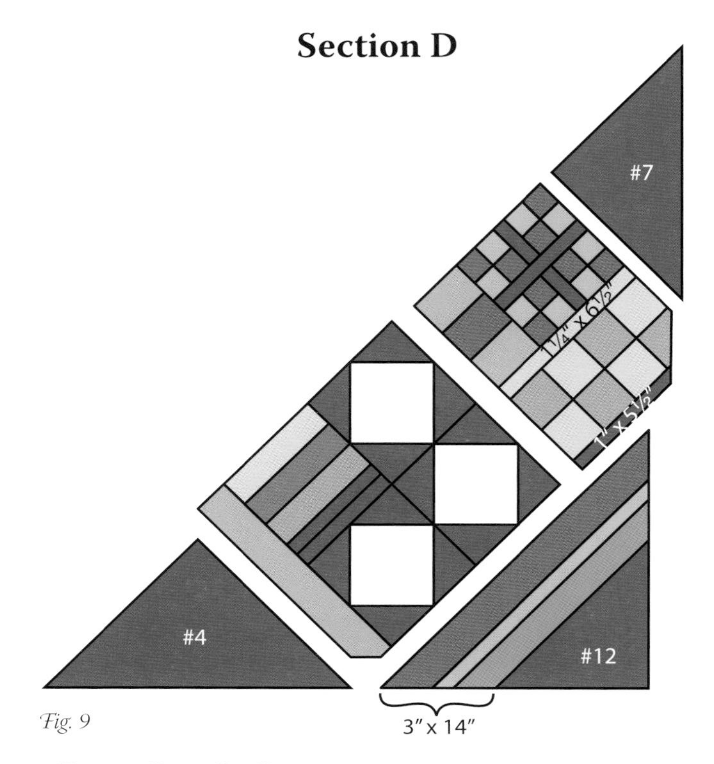

Fig. 9

Four-Patch Cross

Cut 2 strips 1⅜" x 12" from contrasting fabrics and make 4 four-patch units. Join with 1" strips between pairs of four-patches as shown in figure 10. Join the pairs with a 1" x 5" strip. Trim to measure 4½" square.

Cut 3 squares 2" x 2". Sew in a row and add to the cross unit, trimming to fit.

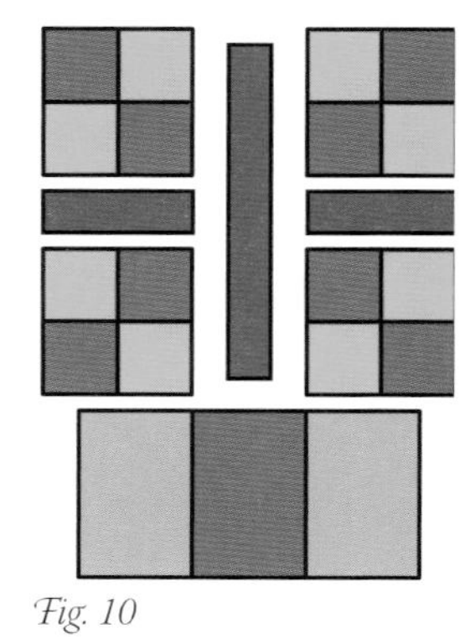

Fig. 10

Checkerboard

Cut 2 strips 2" x 8" and make a 4-segment checkerboard. Cut and add filler strips to both sides as shown in figure 9.

Square-in-a-Square

Cut 5 strips of random widths 4½" long and make a strip-set 4½" wide.

Join with the three 4½" square-in-a-square units and add a filler strip as shown in figure 9.

Join the cross and checkerboard units, then add the square-in-a-square unit. Add setting triangles #4 and #7 aligning the edges as shown in figure 9.

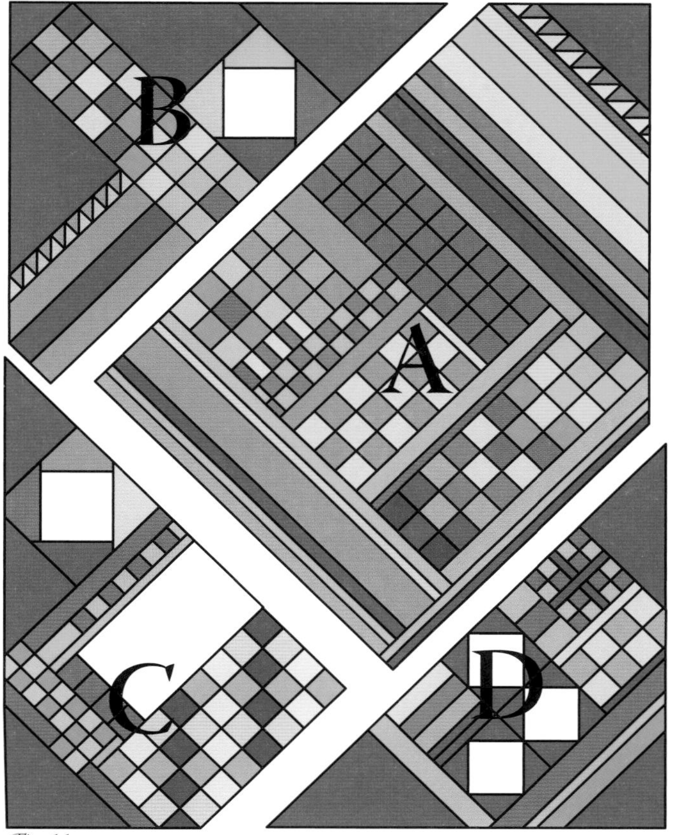

Fig. 11

Filler Strips

Make a 3" wide strip-set of 3 randomly pieced 14" filler strips. Add to the pieced unit as shown. Pin the remaining corner triangle in place to complete section D.

The only thing left to do (other than stand back and admire your quilt) is to join the sections.

Finishing

Join sections A and B. Add section C, aligning the lower edges as shown, and then add section D. Sew the corner triangles in place.

Trim the edges and square up the quilt.

Use the fish pattern and/or cut motifs from your focus fabric and fuse in place following the Fused Appliqué instructions to secure them to your quilt top. Refer to the sample quilt photo for placement ideas.

Layer the quilt top with batting and backing and quilt as desired. Trim the excess backing and batting. Bind with single-fold 1¼" strips.

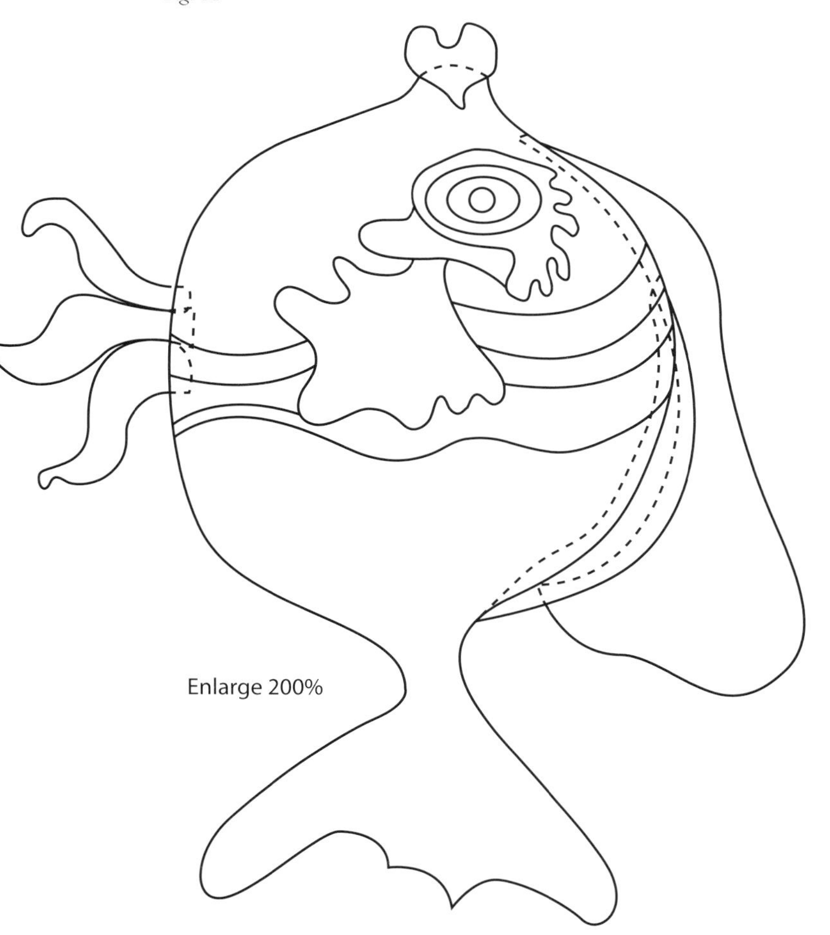

I Give You the Sun, the Moon, and the Stars

32" x 39½", by Jane K. Wells

This wonderful art quilt was created when we discovered the beautiful hand-embroidered fabric squares stitched by women in Haiti. These women use money earned from the sale of their enchanting designs to work their way out of poverty. We figure using their art in ours is a win/win situation. See information on ordering Haitian embroidery on the Resources page.

We made our stars, decided to add other celestial representations, and built the rest of the quilt to become a backdrop for these main blocks. The strip-pieced background is made to represent the sky.

Techniques

Fused Appliqué (page 78)
Half-Square Triangles (page 79)
Lightening Bolt (page 80)
Paper Piecing (page 84)
Star—Paper Pieced Points (page 90)
Star Strip (page 91)
Strip Piecing (page 91)
Zipper (page 93)

Fabric buying tips: We chose bright African prints for the main characters—the sun, the stars, and the moon's facial features. Batiks in sky colors make a nice backdrop to these.

Fabric Requirements & Supplies

3 focus fabric squares 4½" x 4½"
¼ yard or fat eighth of 3 fabrics for the star points
¼ yard or fat eighth for the moon plus scraps for features
7" square for the sun plus ¼ yard gold for rays
¼ yard total of different yellows for the lightning bolt and star strip background
¾ yard total of 12 different deep to medium blues and violets for the strip-pieced sky background
¼ yard fusible web
Batting 36" x 44"
Binding ¼ yard
Backing 1¼ yards

Construction Notes

The quilt is assembled in 2 sections (A and B) that are then sewn together. As you make each component, place it on a design wall in its approximate position while you're making the next. Use the block placement diagrams as a guide.

Remember that you can rearrange or trade out components and fillers any way you want!

Focus Fabric Star Blocks

Cut 8 rectangles 2¾" x 6" for the star points and 8 background squares 4½" x 4½" for each of the 3 stars.

Paper-piece 12 star point units (foundation pattern on page 34). Join with 4½" focus fabric and background squares as shown. Remove the paper.

Variation: Make four-patch blocks from 2½" strips for the corners of the Star blocks.

Section A

Strip-Pieced Setting Triangles

Cut a variety of strips from your background fabrics in a range of widths, from 1" to 2¾" wide. Make strip-sets and cut right-angle triangles as indicated.

Fig. 1

Note that sometimes the strips are parallel to the triangle legs and sometimes parallel to the hypotenuse. Label the triangles.

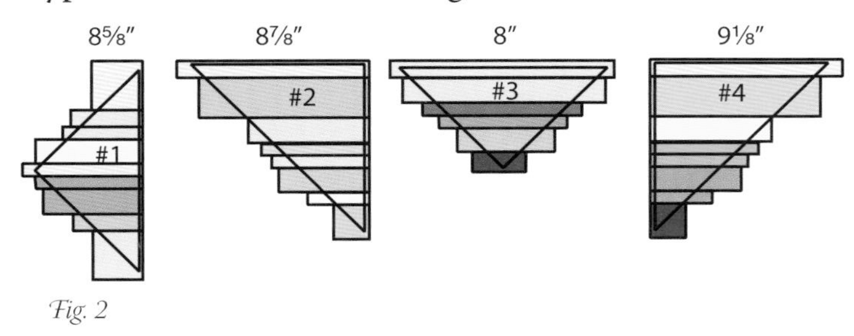

Fig. 2

Join two star blocks, the setting triangles, and a filler strip as shown in figure 1. Trim the corners as shown.

Half-Square Triangles

Make 16 half-square triangles from 2¾" x 22" strips. Trim to measure 2¼" square. Sew in a strip as shown in figure 1.

Five-Star Strip

Cut fabrics for the five-star strip as shown.

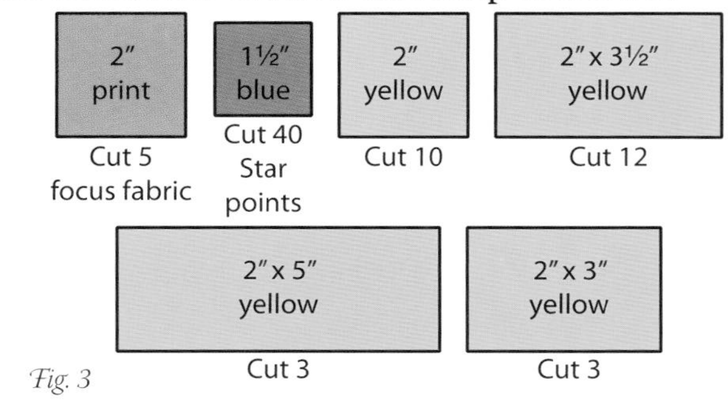

Fig. 3

Make the star point units.

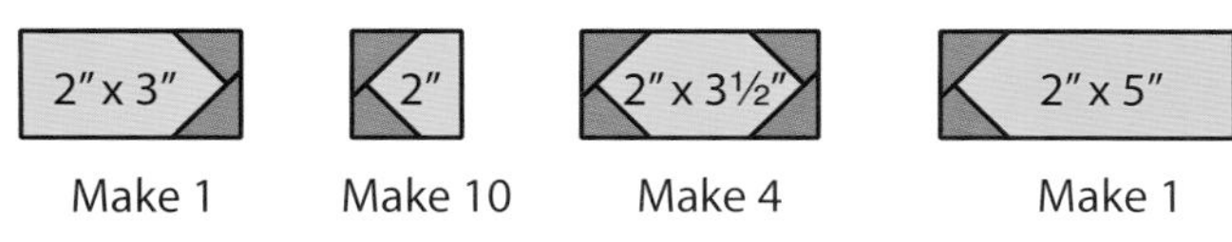

Fig. 4

Arrange the pieces as shown, sew into rows, then join the rows. The right edge of the star strip will be trimmed at a diagonal later.

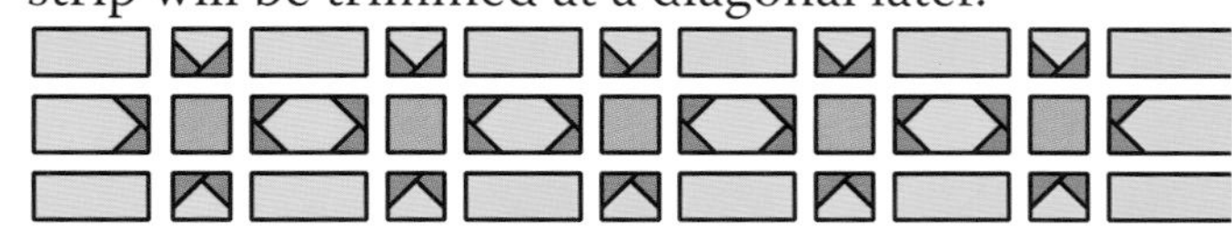

Fig. 5

Variation: Fussy cut the 2" squares to feature a fabric design motif in each of the stars.

Zipper

Cut 2 contrasting strips 1½" x 39" into segments 17" and 22" long. Make an 11-segment zipper with the 17" strips and border with the 22" strips.

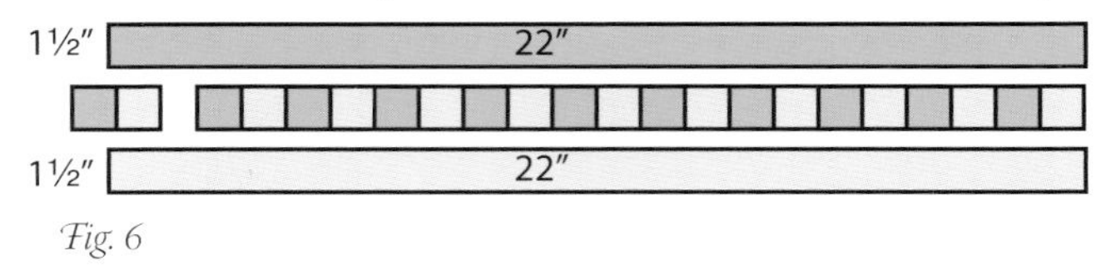

Fig. 6

Join the half-square triangles, five-star strip, and zipper unit, aligning the edges as shown in figure 1.

Paper-Pieced Sun

Enlarge the sun paper-piecing foundation and sun center (page 35). Trace the sun center onto the dull side of freezer paper. Paper piece the sun rays in the sequence shown on the foundation. Press the sun center freezer paper to the fabric. Transfer registration marks and remove the freezer paper.

Join the sun rays with the sun center. Trim along the cutting lines and remove the paper.

Add the sun to the zipper unit. Square up this corner of the quilt top, trimming off the ends of the zipper/star/triangle unit.

Sky Background and Moon

Make 12 nine-patch units from a variety of 2" strips. Cut two nine-patches in half diagonally and arrange with the other 10. Sew into rows, then join the rows. Trim at a 45-degree angle, with the upper left side measuring 22" as shown.

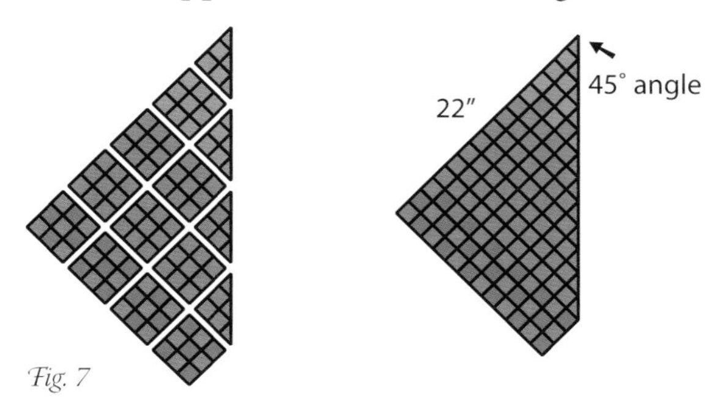

Fig. 7

Appliqué the moon (page 34) onto the nine-patch background.

Add to the focus fabric star unit.

Join with the sun/zipper/star/triangle unit to complete section A.

Section B

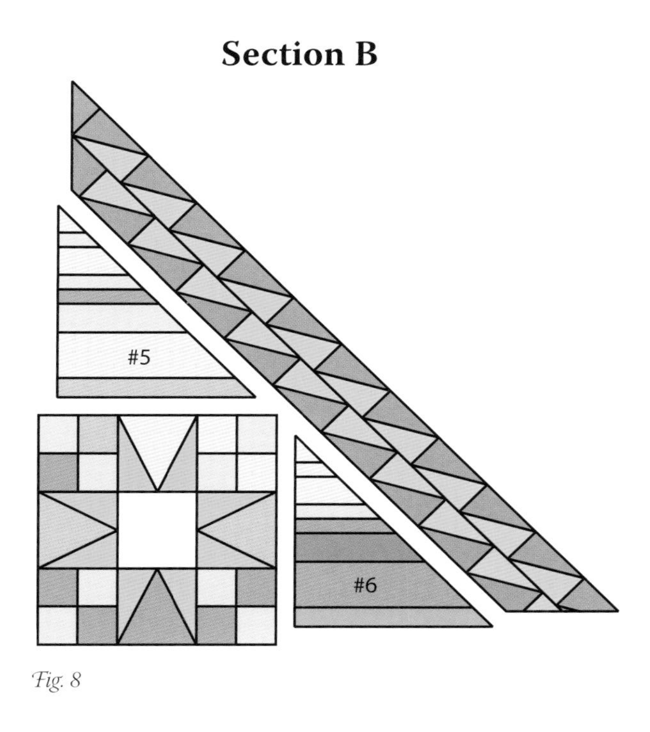

Fig. 8

Strip-Pieced Setting Triangles

Cut a variety of strips from your background in a range of widths, from 1" to 2¾" wide. Make a strip-set and cut 2 right triangles as shown.

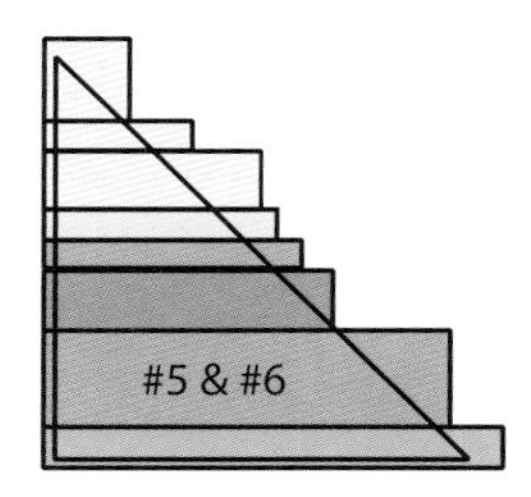

Fig. 9

Join the triangles with the remaining Star block as shown in figure 8.

Lightning Bolt

Cut 10 rectangles 2½" x 4½" from each of two contrasting fabrics and make a 20-unit Lightning Bolt strip. Add fillers as shown.

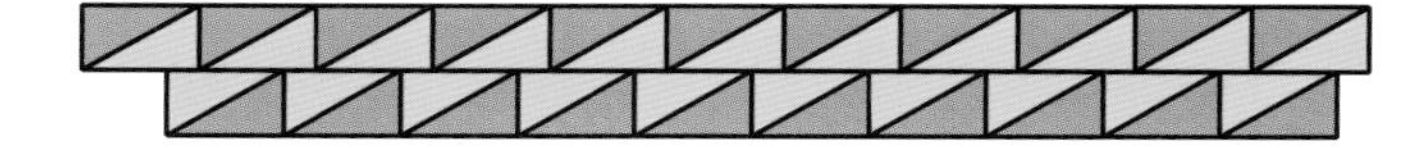

Fig. 10

Join with the Star block to complete section B.

That's all there is to section B. You're almost done!

Finishing

Join sections A and B. Square up the quilt top. Layer the quilt top with batting and backing and quilt as desired. Trim the excess backing and batting. Bind with single-fold 1¼" strips.

Fig. 11

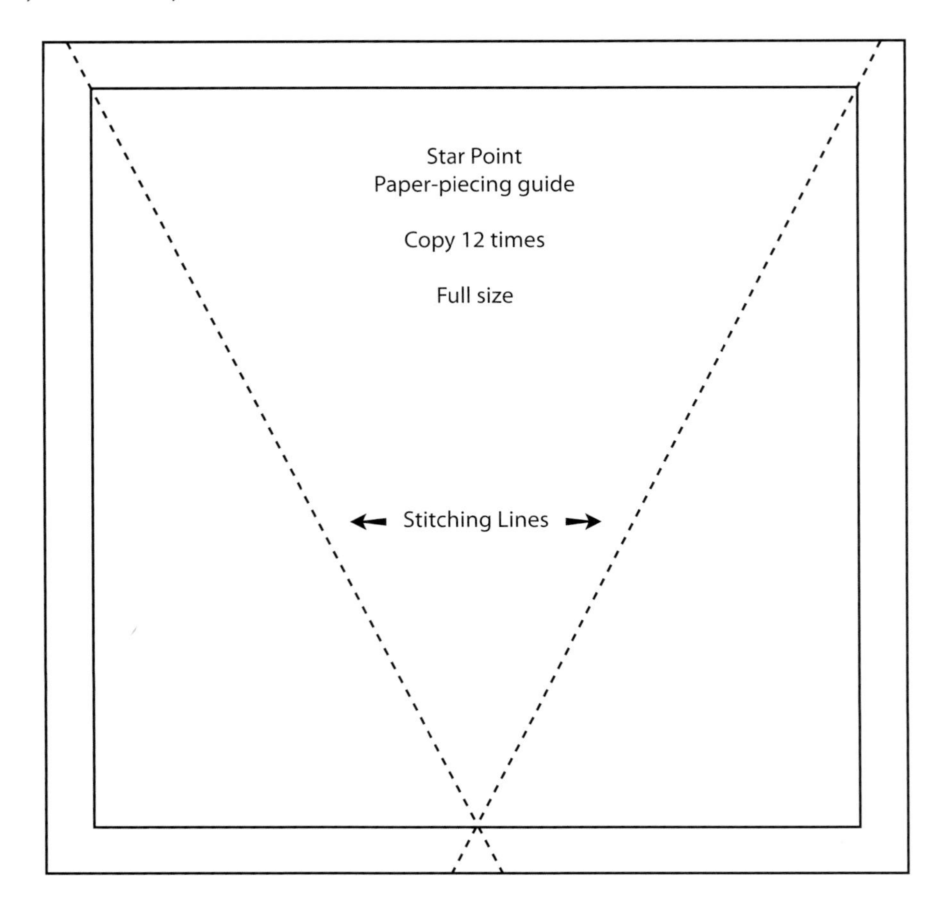
Star Point
Paper-piecing guide
Copy 12 times
Full size
Stitching Lines

I Give You the
Sun, the Moon
and the Stars
Trace this reversed
image to the fusible web.
Enlarge 200%

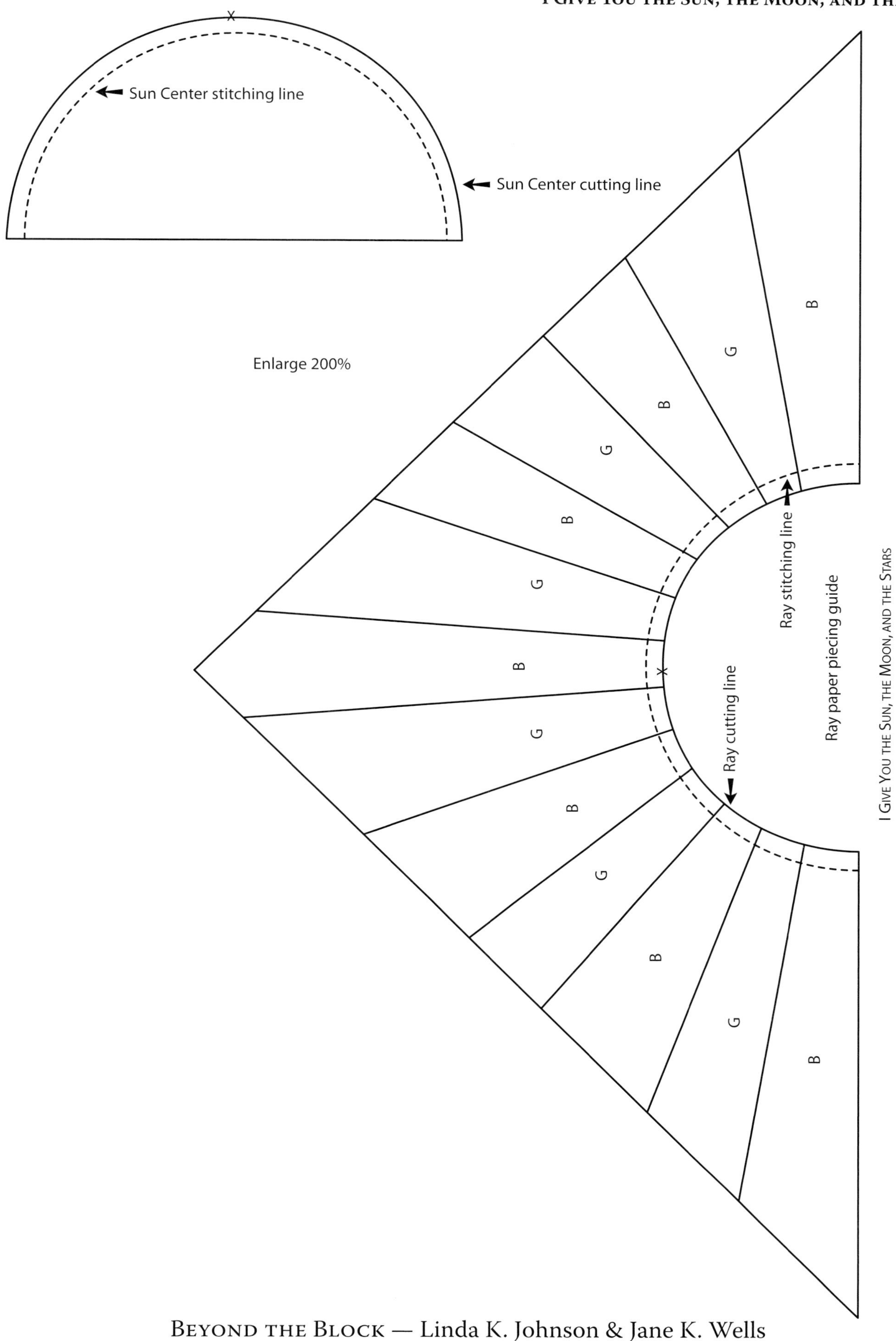
Sun Center stitching line
Sun Center cutting line
Enlarge 200%
B
G
B
G
B
G
B
G
B
G
B
G
B
Ray stitching line
Ray cutting line
Ray paper piecing guide
I Give You the Sun, the Moon, and the Stars

Guatemala en Rojo

43" x 41", pieced and quilted by Jane K. Wells

This little quilt started with the delightful center appliqué that was an experiment using hand woven Guatemalan striped fabric with machine blanket stitch. The solid red fabric is silk, which we think beautifully complements the coarser weave of the Guatemalan stripes. If you don't want to do the appliqué, you could choose a special large print, a needlepoint or four smaller squares as your center and build around that. One of our pattern testers appliquéd a fantastic Dresden Plate—you are limited only by your imagination.

Enlarge 200%

Summer

56" x 46", pieced and quilted by Jane K. Wells

Sunshine and summer, flowers and butterflies—what a wonderful feeling. We used gloriously warm colors to conjure up the fabulous mood of summer. This quilt is relatively simple but an arty feel abounds. Note that we often used a fabulous yellow-green that goes from light to dark on the same bolt. THANKS fabric designers! We decided to add a 5" border so that it is just large enough to use as a lap quilt on those cooler summer evenings when a light quilt makes summer reading just delicious. Other colors can depict another mood just as excitingly.

Techniques

Borders (page 72)
Broken Dishes (page 73)
Checkerboard (page 73)
Flower Basket (page 76)
Flying Geese (page 76)
Friendship Star (page 77)
Fused Appliqué (page 78)
Half-Square Triangles (page 79)
Mitered Border (page 82)
Mitered-Square Triangles (page 83)
Setting Triangles (page 87)
Square-in-a-Square (page 88)
Star—Ohio (page 89)
Strip Piecing (page 91)
Zipper (page 93)

Fabric Requirements & Supplies

Use several different values of each of these colors to total yardage given:

½ yard greens
½ yard yellows to oranges (our background colors)
⅓ yard light to dark violet
¼ yard print for butterfly wings
½ yard large scale florals (6"–7" motifs) fabrics
¼ yard of 4 different stripes (1 yard total)
¼ yard fusible webbing
¼ yard for optional inner border
1¼ yard stripes for optional outer border
Batting 64" x 54"
Backing and hanging sleeve 3½ yards
Binding ¼ yard

Construction Notes

The quilt is assembled in 4 sections (A, B, C, and D) that are then sewn together. As you make each component, place it on a design wall in its approximate position while you're making the next. Use the block placement diagrams as a guide.

Remember that you can rearrange or trade out components and fillers any way you want!

Fabric Buying and Using Tips

As always, having dark, medium, and light values makes your quilt more interesting. We love the effect many different stripes have, with prints added sparingly for more interest.

Section A

Square-in-a-Square

Cut 4 flower focus fabric squares 4½" x 4½" and 4 strips 3¼" x 17" of striped fabric.

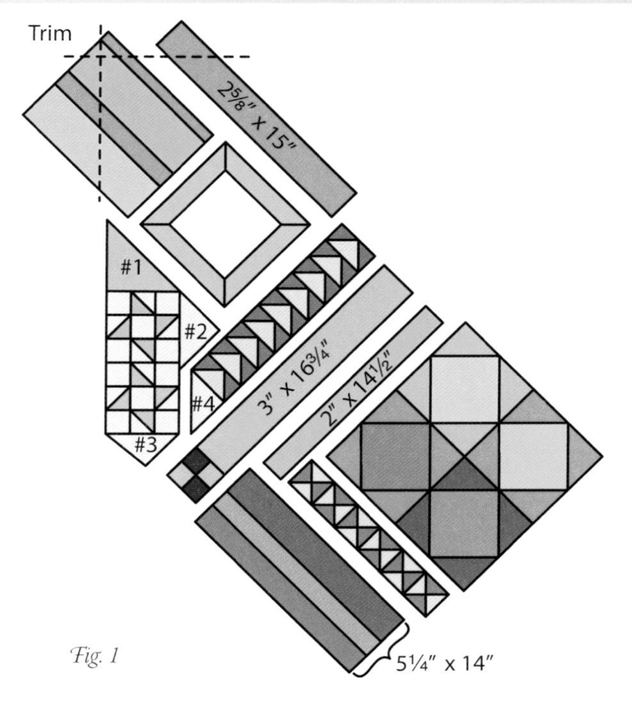

Fig. 1

Use a 4½" square ruler to cut 4 right-angle triangles from each of 4 striped fabrics.

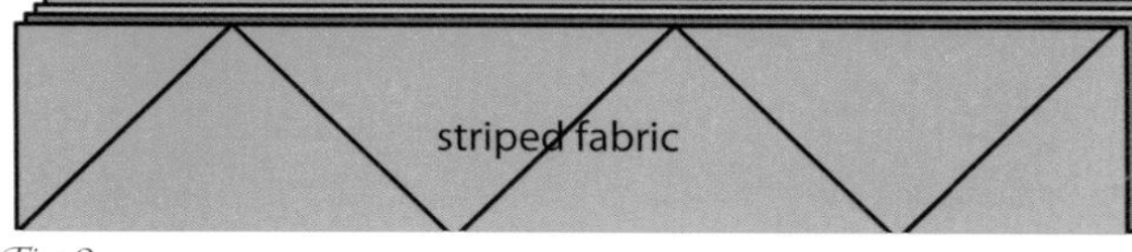

Fig. 2

Follow the Square-in-a-Square instructions adding 4 matching triangles to each focus fabric square. Trim each to measure 6½" square and join in a four-patch arrangement as shown in figure 1.

Broken Dishes

Cut 2 strips 3½" x 15" from contrasting fabrics and make 8 Broken Dishes units. Trim to measure 2½" square. Sew 6 together in a strip. Set aside the seventh for section C. (You'll have one unit left over.)

Add the Broken Dishes strip and a filler strip to the other joined units as shown in figure 1.

Strip-Set

Make a strip-set 5¼" x 29¼" and cut in two segments, 14" and 15¼" long. Sew the shorter segment to the Broken Dishes/square-in-a-square unit. Set aside the longer segment for section C.

Four-Patch

Make 7 four-patch units from 2" x 26½" strips of contrasting fabric. Sew 1 four-patch unit to the end of a filler strip and add to section A as shown in figure 1.

Set aside the remaining 6 four-patch units for section C.

Friendship Star

Cut 3 center and 12 background squares 2" x 2" and 6 squares each of background and star point fabrics 2⅞" x 2⅞". Make 3 Friendship Star blocks. Join 2 blocks and set aside the remaining block for Section D.

Setting Triangles

Cut a 5⅛" square in half on the diagonal. Trim one triangle so the legs are 4⅛". Cut a 3½" square in half on the diagonal. Label the triangles as shown.

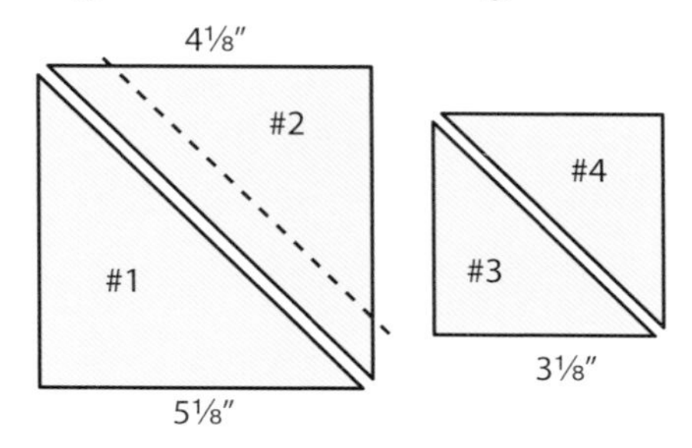

Fig. 3

Add triangles #1, #2, and #3 to the Friendship Star blocks as shown in figure 1.

Flying Geese

Cut 9 rectangles 2" x 3¼" and 18 squares 2" x 2" and make a strip of 9 Flying Geese units. Add setting triangle #4 to the end as shown in figure 1.

Framed Flower

Cut a 5½" square of focus fabric. Add a mitered border of 1¾" x 10" strips. Trim to 7¾" square.

Make a strip-set 7¾" x 8¾". Add to the framed flower unit, then add a 2⅝" x 15" strip as shown in figure 1.

Completing Section A

Join the framed square unit to the Friendship Star unit. Join with the Flying Geese strip, making a Y seam at setting triangle #4. Join with the previously completed unit to complete section A.

Lookin' good!

Section B

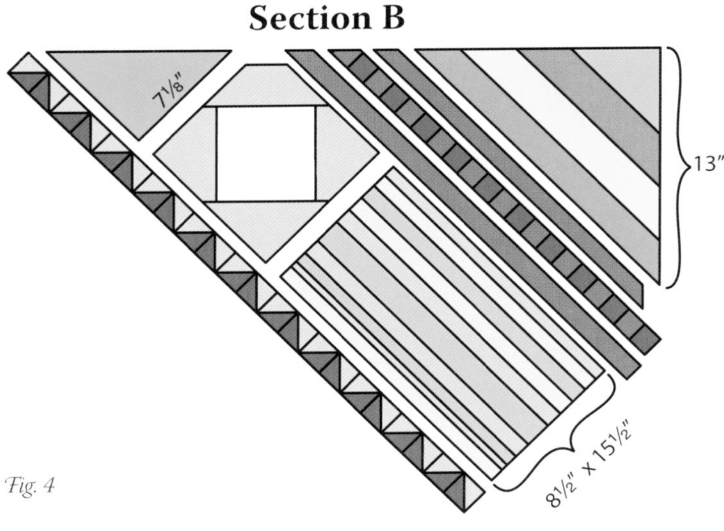

Fig. 4

Half-Square Triangles

Cut 1 strip 2½" x 28" from 2 contrasting fabrics and make 22 half-square triangles. Trim to measure 2" square. Join in a strip, alternating the placement of the darker fabric as shown in figure 4.

Strip Piecing

Make a strip-set and trim to 8½" x 15½" as a background for the butterflies.

Square-in-a-Square

Cut a focus fabric square 5½" x 5½". Cut 4 mitered square triangles using a 5½" square ruler and frame the focus fabric square. Trim to measure 8½" square. Join with the strip-pieced background.

Cut and add a right-angle setting triangle as shown in figure 4

Appliqué 3 butterflies on the strip-pieced section. (Templates are on page 47.)

Zipper

Cut 2 constrasting strips 1½" x 21" for the zipper teeth and 1½" x 27" strips to border them.

Strip-Pieced Setting Triangle

Strip piece a unit at least 9" x 18½" and cut a right-angle triangle with 13" legs.

Join with the other units to complete section B.

Section B is done! We never doubted you.

Section C

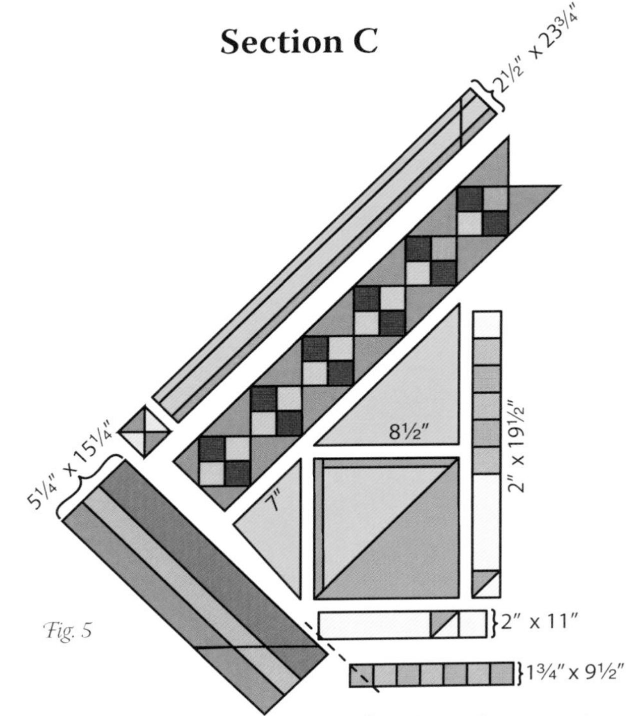

Fig. 5

Add a filler strip or strip-pieced unit to the remaining Broken Dishes unit as shown in figure 5.

Squares-on-Point

Cut a strip 6" x 34" of striped fabric. Cut 14 mitered triangles using a 4" square ruler. Make a Squares-on-Point strip with the 6 remaining four-patch units (from section A) as the center squares. Trim to 4¾" wide. Join with the Broken Dishes/filler strips unit. (Use as many as needed to fit.)

Flower Basket

Make a Flower Basket block and trim to measure 8¼" square.

Fillers

Add right-angle filler triangles to the Flower Basket as shown in figure 5.

Make 2 half-square triangles with 2 squares 2⅞" x 2⅞". Piece 2" squares and 2" wide rectangles into 2 filler strips and add to the Flower Basket unit, aligning the half-square triangles as shown in figure 5 for the basket base.

Trim as shown and add to the four-patch square-in-a-square unit.

Make a checkerboard with 1¾" squares and join with the basket base. Trim.

Add the longer strip-pieced segment from section A to complete section C.

Done! Fini! Just one more small section left to tackle.

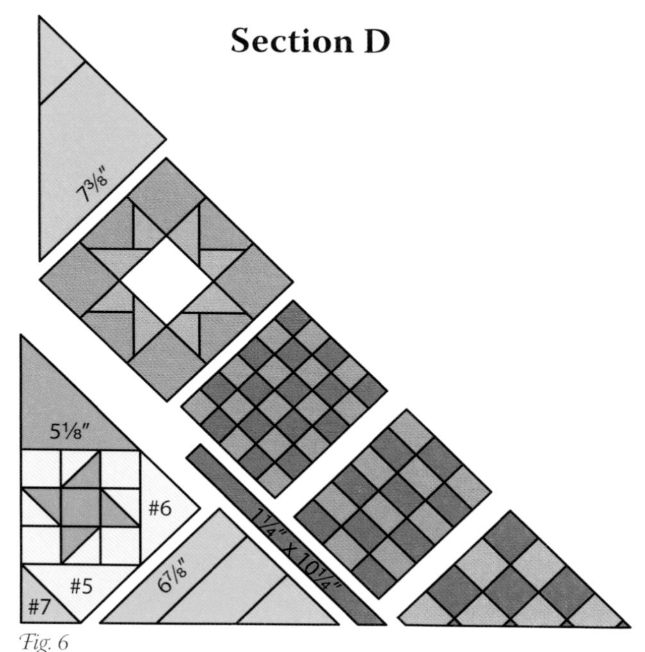

Fig. 6

Ohio Star

Cut a 3¼" center square, 4 rectangles 2½" x 3¼", 4 squares 2½" x 2½" from background fabric, and eight 2½" squares for the star points. Make an Ohio Star block.

Add a plain or pieced right-angle setting triangle with the hypotenuse on the straight-of-grain as shown in figure 6.

Checkerboards

Cut 2 strips 1½" x 23" from contrasting fabrics. Make a checkerboard with 5 rows of three 1½" segments each.

Cut 2 strips 1½" x 18" from contrasting fabrics. Make a checkerboard with 3 rows of three 2" segments each.

Cut 2 strips 2" x 16" from contrasting fabrics. Make a checkerboard with 4½ rows of two 2" segments each.

Join the 3 checkerboard units with a filler strip as shown in figure 6.

Friendship Star

Cut 2 squares in half on the diagonal and label as shown. Cut a pieced right-angle triangle with 6⅞" legs as shown in figure 6.

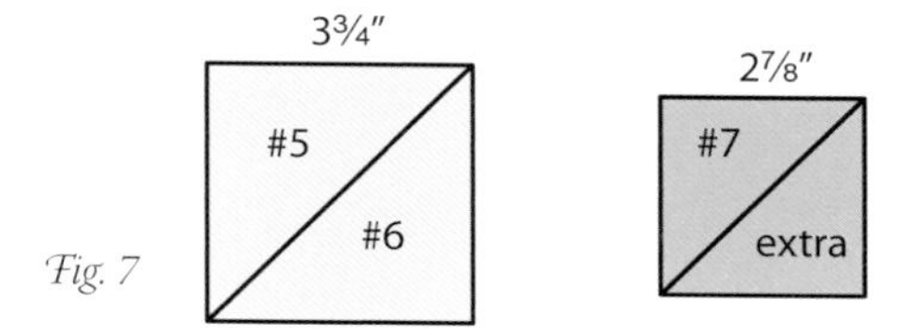

Fig. 7

Add the setting triangles to the remaining Friendship Star block as shown in figure 6 and join with the checkerboard units to complete section D.

Finishing

Join sections A and B. Add section C, then section D and square up the quilt top.

For optional inner and mitered borders, cut 1½" strips from the inner border fabric. Add them to the quilt. Cut 5½" strips from the striped outer border fabric and add to the quilt, mitering the corners.

Add appliqués of motifs cut from your floral fabric as desired.

Layer the quilt top with batting and backing and quilt as desired. Trim the excess backing and batting. Bind with single-fold 1¼" strips.

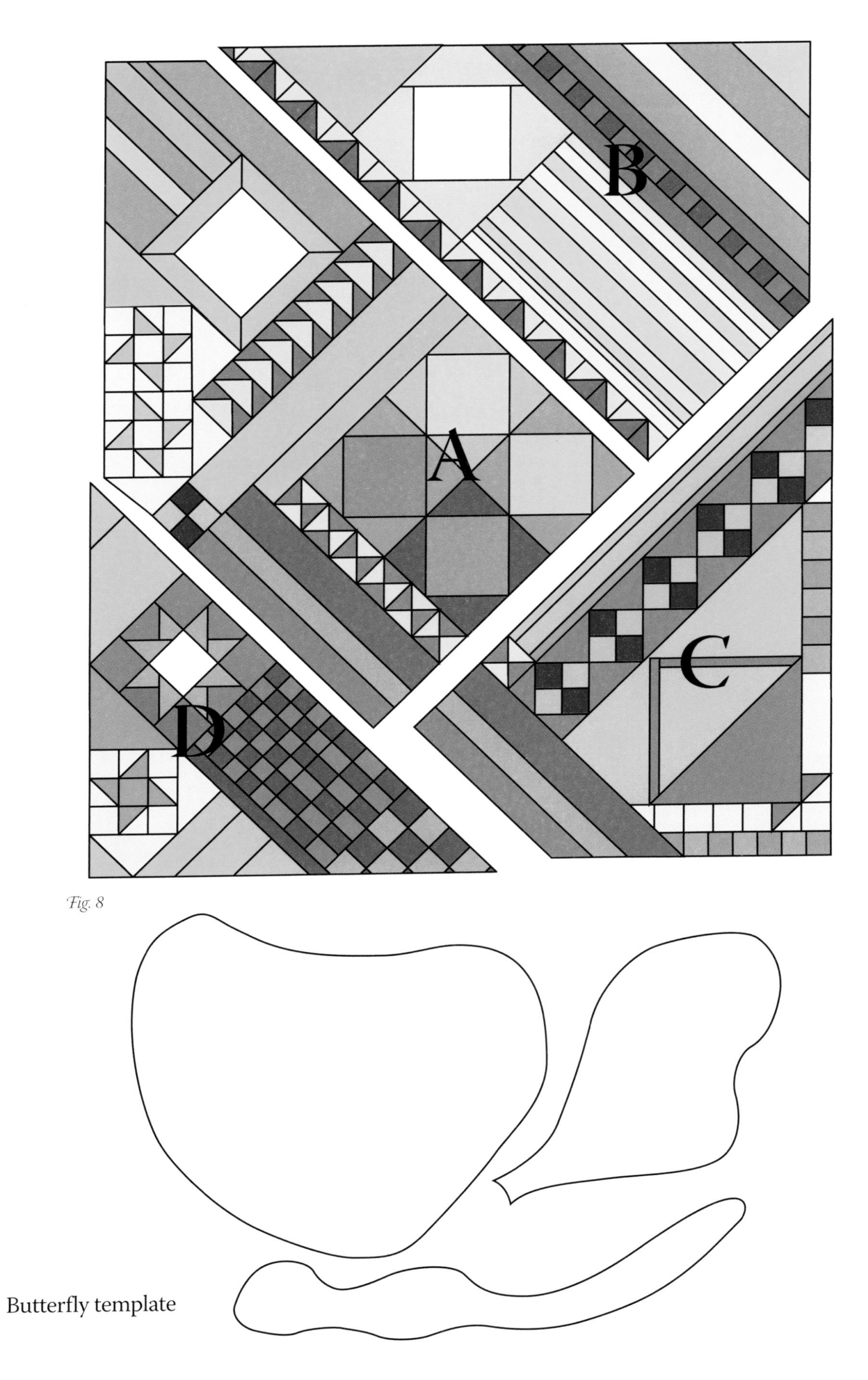

Fig. 8

Butterfly template

Ah, Autumn!

42" x 57", pieced and quilted by Linda K. Johnson

This stunning quilt was inspired by the brilliant fall colors of Indiana. Hand-woven Guatemalan cotton was used for the striped leaves. This Guatemalan fabric adds richness and the mottled batik fabric adds sparkle. Note how the assortment of bright and muted colors in light, medium, and dark values creates luminosity. A few large prints are mixed with smaller prints. Imagine how beautiful this might play in spring or summer colors.

Zipper Variation

Make a strip-set with 2 strips 1" x 32". Cut 15 segments 1½" wide and 2 segments 2½" wide. Alternate with 16 squares 1½" x 1½" for the zipper teeth, putting the longer segments at the ends. Border the teeth with 1½" x 39½" strips

Add filler strips as shown in figure 8 on page 52.

Setting Triangles

Cut 2 squares 7" x 7" in half on the diagonal. Arrange 3 triangles with the remaining 3 Maple Leaf blocks as shown, alternating the position of the stems. Sew into rows and join the rows together.

Join with the zipper and filler strips to complete section D.

Finishing

Join sections A and B. Add section C, then section D and square up the quilt top.

Layer the quilt top with batting and backing and quilt as desired. Trim the excess backing and batting. Bind with single-fold 1¼" strips.

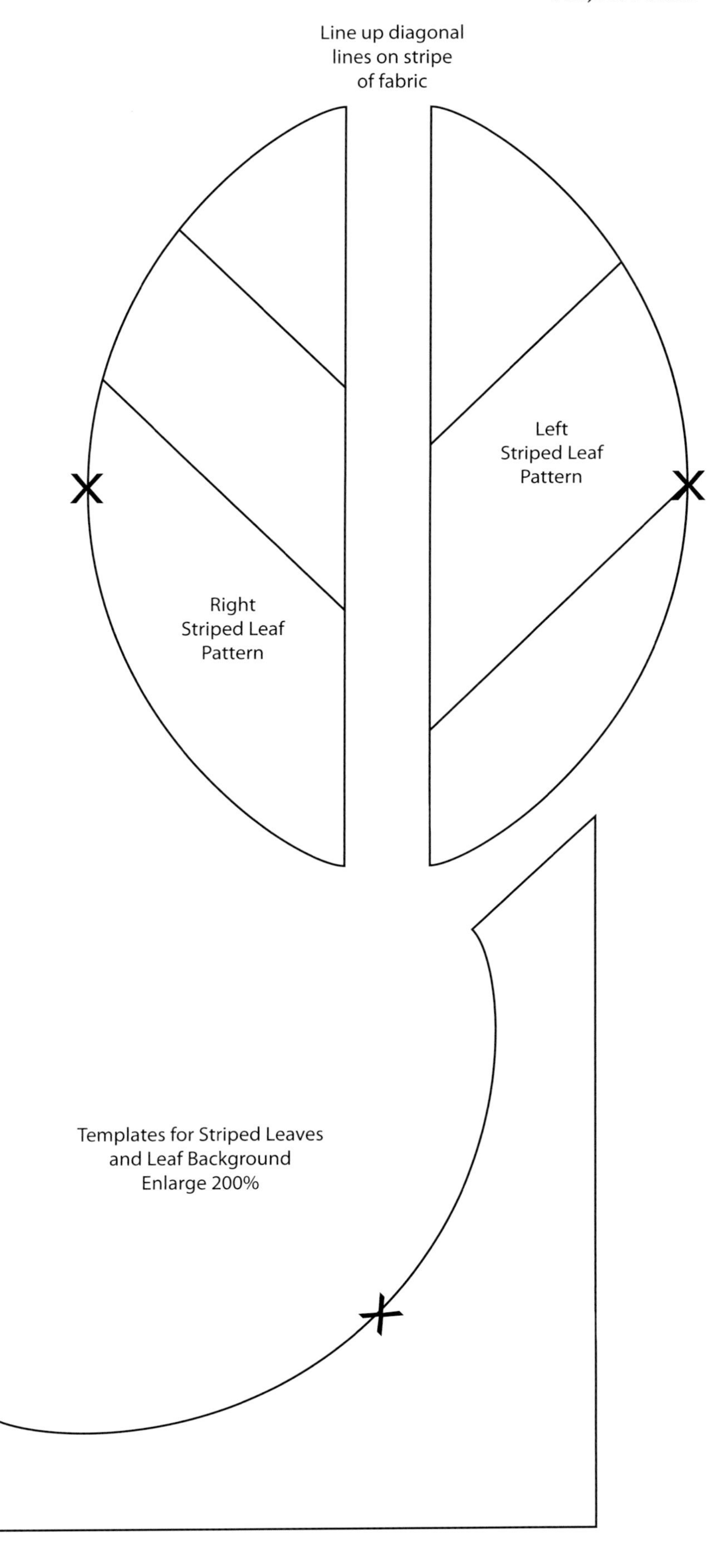

Front Yard Gardens

37" x 50", pieced and quilted by Jane K. Wells

These colors remind me of the front yards of many neighboring Amish farms. There usually is a beautiful flower garden filled with bright oranges, yellows, and reds of zinnias as well as shades of violet Bee Balm, red roses, and an assortment of vegetables. In the side yard, less brightly colored clothes flutter in the breeze on wash day. The solid colors with subtle and high contrasts greatly enhance the graphic appeal.

Techniques

Bias Vines (page 72)
Borders (page 72)
Chevron Strips (page 74)
Flying Geese (page 76)
Four-Patch (page 77)
Log Cabin, half variation (page 81)
Half-Square Triangles from Squares (page 79)
Squares-on-Point Strip (page 88)
Strip Piecing (page 91)

Fabric Requirements & Supplies

1½ yards background or 5 fat quarters for a scrappy background
1 yard total assorted scraps for flowers
¼ yard greens for stems
1½ yards several shades of flower fabrics and zingers
¼ yard for 1½" border strips
1⅝ yards backing and hanging sleeve
39" x 56" batting
¼ yard for single-fold binding
¼" and ⅜" bias bars

Construction Notes

The quilt is assembled in 4 sections (A, B, C, and D) that are then sewn together. As you make each component, place it on a design wall in its approximate position while you're making the next. Use the block placement diagrams as a guide.

Remember that you can rearrange or trade out components and fillers any way you want!

Section A

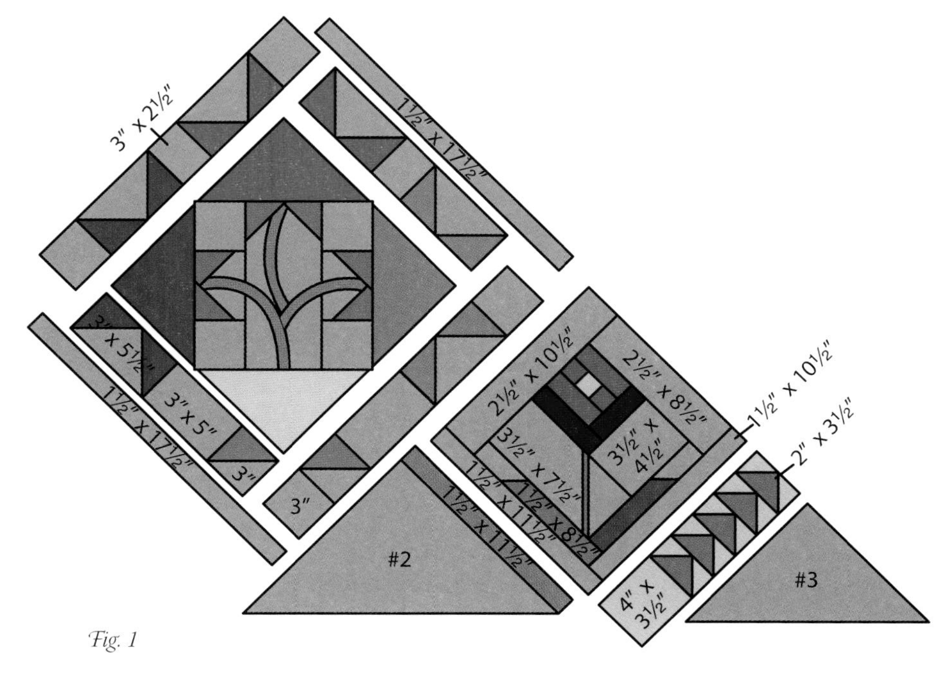

Fig. 1

Posy Block 1

Cut 6 green squares 2½" x 2½" and 3 background pieces 3" x 4", 3" x 4", and 9" x 4". Piece 3 Flying Geese units as shown in figure 2. Add 4 corner squares and join for the central leaf unit.

3" x 3"
2½"
3" x 4"
2½"
3" x 3"
2½"
4" x 9"

Fig. 2

Add right-angle triangles with 7" legs and make a square-in-a-square with the leaf unit as the center square.

Make 2 Flying Geese petals for each of the three flowers from 3" x 5½" rectangles and 3" x 3" squares. Make 2 half-square triangles from 4" squares for the base of the basket. Trim half-square triangles to measure 3" square.

Add the Flying Geese, half-square triangles, corner squares, and fillers as shown in figure 1.

Add a border of 1½" strips to two sides of block 1 as shown in figure 1.

Make ⅜" bias stems from a strip 1¼" x 22" and cut into 3 segments: 8½", 7", and 6½". See the sample quilt photo for placement. Turn under the ends of the stems or pick a few stitches and tuck the stems under the flower leaves and vase. Appliqué the stems in place. Sew the openings closed, catching the stems in the seams.

Posy Block 2

Make a modified Log Cabin block as shown in figure 3 with a 1½" center and 1½" wide logs.

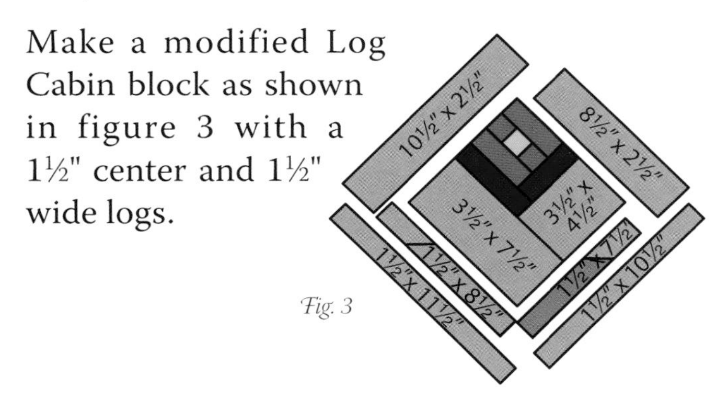

Fig. 3

Add fillers as shown. To make the leaf fillers, join strips of background and leaf fabrics with a diagonal seam, then cut the strip to the size indicated in figure 3.

Make a ¼" wide stem 6" long and appliqué in place as shown in figure 1.

Flying Geese

There are 3 sets of Flying Geese, one in Section A and two in Section B. You'll need a total of 18 rectangles 2" x 3½" and 36 squares 2" x 2". Make 18 Flying Geese units. Join 5 units in a strip with a filler as shown in figure 1 and add to Posy block 2 (fig. 1).

Set aside the remaining Flying Geese units for section B.

Setting Triangles

Cut one corner and six side setting triangles from two 12½" squares. Label the triangles.

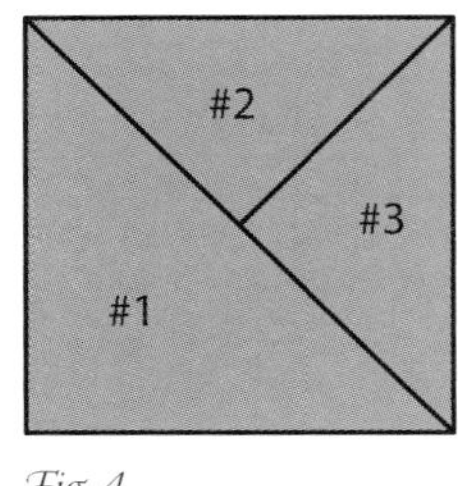

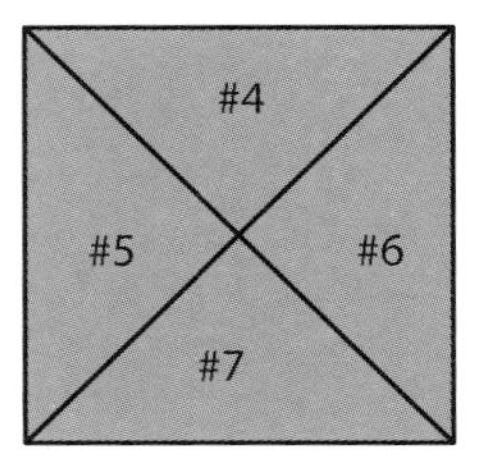

Fig. 4

Add a filler strip to triangle #2 as shown in figure 1.

Join the Posy blocks, Flying Geese strip, and setting triangles #2 and #3 to complete section A.

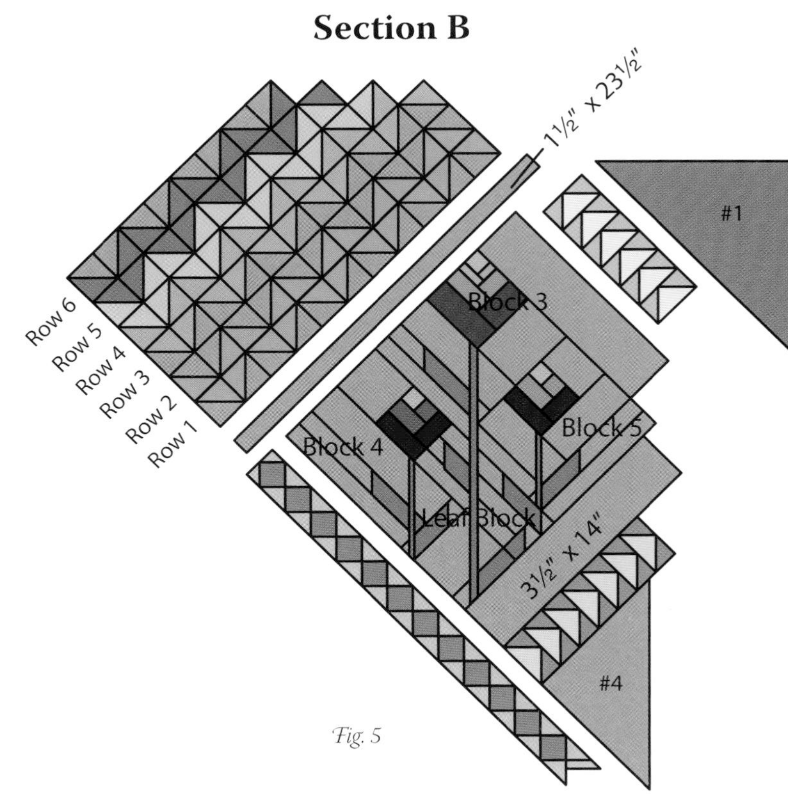

Fig. 5

Squares-on-Point

Cut 12 center squares 2" x 2" and 6 background squares 3½" x 3½" to make a 12-unit squares-on-point strip.

Half-Square Triangle Zigzag

Make half-square triangles from 3" squares, trim each to measure 2½" square. There are 2 colors in each row, but use more than 1 fabric per color to get the 3-D look.

Rows 1 & 2	12 squares from background & color 1	make 24
Row 3	6 squares from background & color 2	make 11
Row 4	5 squares from colors 2 & 3	make 10
Row 5	5 squares from colors 3 & 4	make 9
Row 6	4 squares from background & color 4	make 8

Sew the half-square triangles into rows, orienting them as shown in the sample quilt photo.

Join the rows and a filler strip as shown in figure 5.

Posy Blocks 3, 4, and 5

Make 3 half-Log Cabin blocks as shown in figure 6.

Add filler strips and leaf & background strips as shown in figure 6.

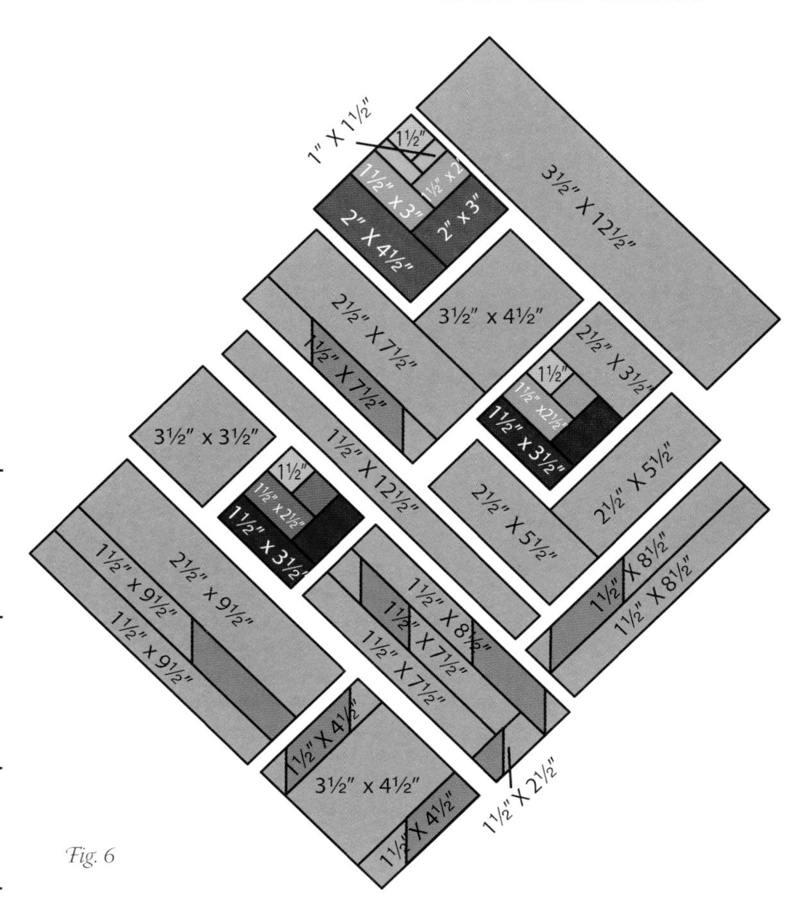

Fig. 6

To add a second point to a leaf, sew a square of background fabric with a diagonal seam to the end of the leaf portion of the trimmed strip as shown. Trim the seam allowance and press.

Join the Posy and Leaf blocks as shown in figure 5.

Join the remaining Flying Geese into rows of 6 and 7 units each. Add these units, the fillers, the squares-on-point strip, and setting triangles #1 and #4.

Appliqué ¼" bias stems in place to complete section B. See the sample quilt photo on page 54 for placement ideas.

Section C

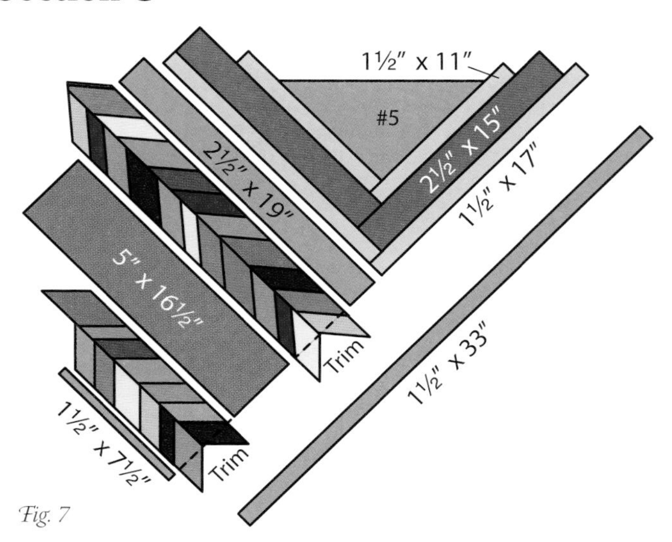

Fig. 7

Section D

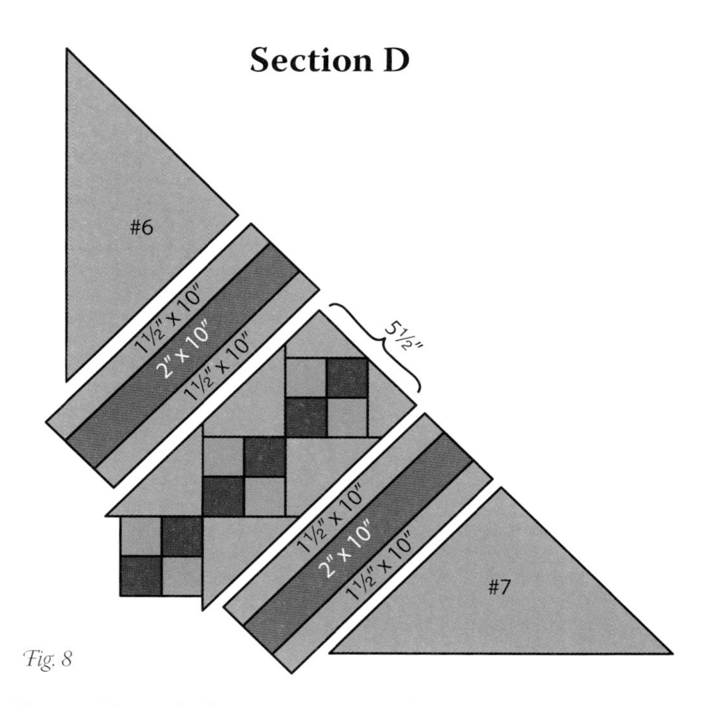

Fig. 8

Chevron Strips

Cut about 30 strips 1" to 2" wide and 9½" long from a variety of different fabrics.

Make 2 strip-sets at least 19" long and cut 2 segments 2½" wide from each strip-set. Join into 2 chevrons, trimming one end straight as shown in figure 7.

Half-Log Cabin

Make a half-Log Cabin block using setting triangle #5 as the center "square" as shown in figure 7. Trim to a right-angle triangle with 17" legs.

Join with filler strips and chevrons as shown in figure 7 to complete section C.

We'd say section C was almost too easy. Only one more easy section to go!

Four-Patch Squares-on-Point

Make 3 four-patch units with 2" x 12" strips.

Cut 2 squares 7" x 7" twice on the diagonal and make a squares-on-point strip with the four-patch units as the center squares. Trim this strip to measure 5½" wide.

Make the fillers as shown in Fig. 8.

Join the squares-on-point unit, fillers, and setting triangles #6 and #7 to complete section D.

Finishing

Join sections A and B. Add section C, then section D, and square up the quilt top. Add a border of 1½" strips.

Layer the quilt top with batting and backing and quilt as desired. There's plenty of room for wonderful quilting. Trim the excess backing and batting. Bind with single-fold 1¼" strips.

Don't forget to add a label and love your quilt!

Fig. 9

Friendship Garden

37" x 50", pieced and quilted by Linda K. Johnson

A great variety of background fabrics makes the different sections of this quilt more obvious. Softer colors in homespun plaids mix well with the large and small floral prints to give this quilt a country look. The whole secret of this quilt's success is its fantastic value placement and the mix of warm and cool colors.

Christmas

37" x 37", pieced and quilted by Jane K. Wells

We love red and green Christmas quilts, especially enjoying how these colors are the perfect complement for each other. There is such an awesome array of Christmas fabric available now and we were delighted to find the blue Christmas fabric throw in as a wow factor. This pattern showcases a couple of great theme fabrics that guided our choices of colors and fabrics for the supporting and filler blocks. Notice how the white adds sparkle.

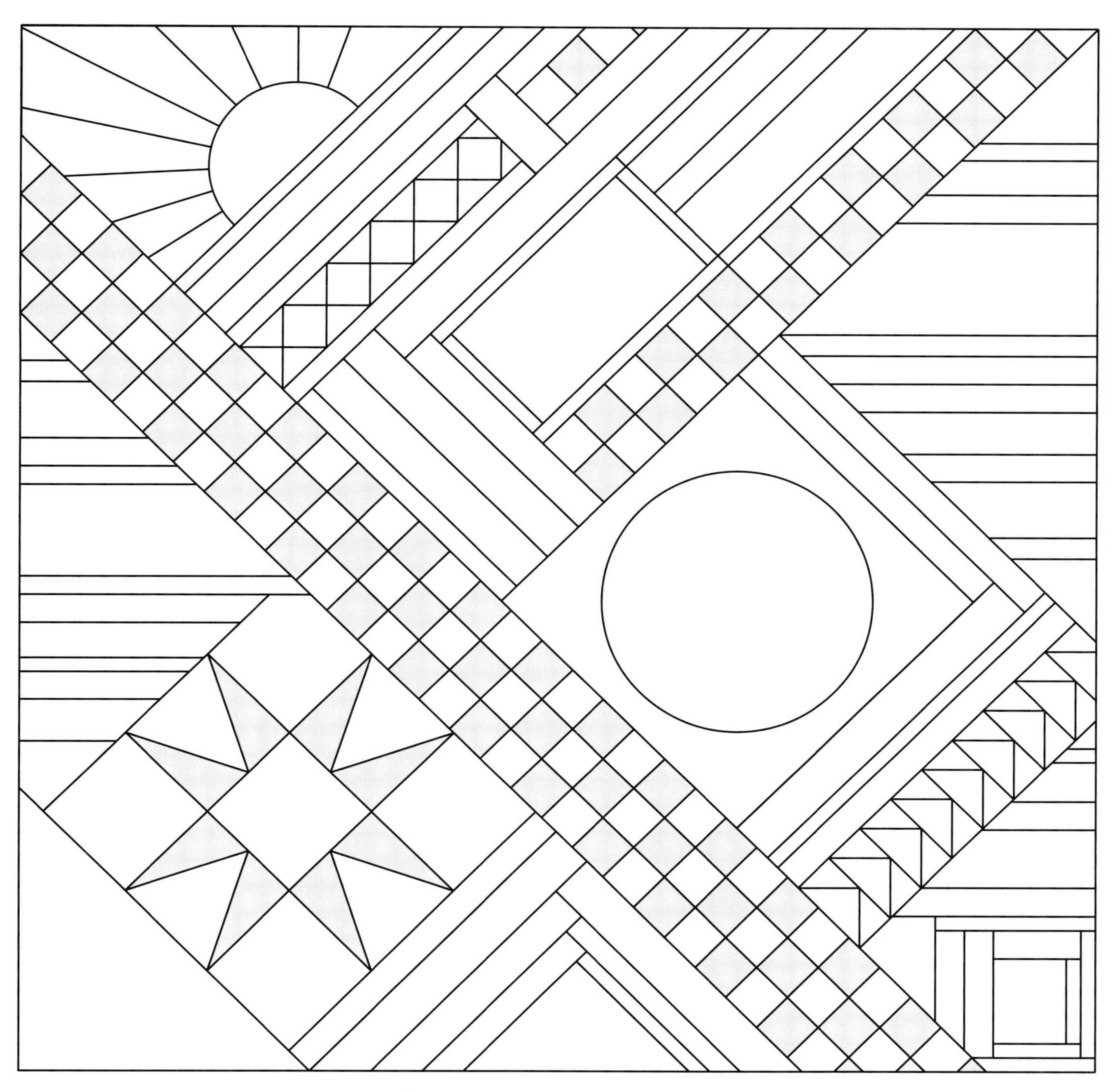

Block Placement diagram for
Christmas

This quilt features the Circle in a Square technique.
See page 74 for complete directions.

Let It Snow

41" x 57", pieced and quilted by Linda K. Johnson

You can choose any theme print to suit your fancy and build a quilt around that theme with many different easy-to-piece blocks. This makes a nice winter wallhanging, or back it in flannel for a cozy lap quilt.

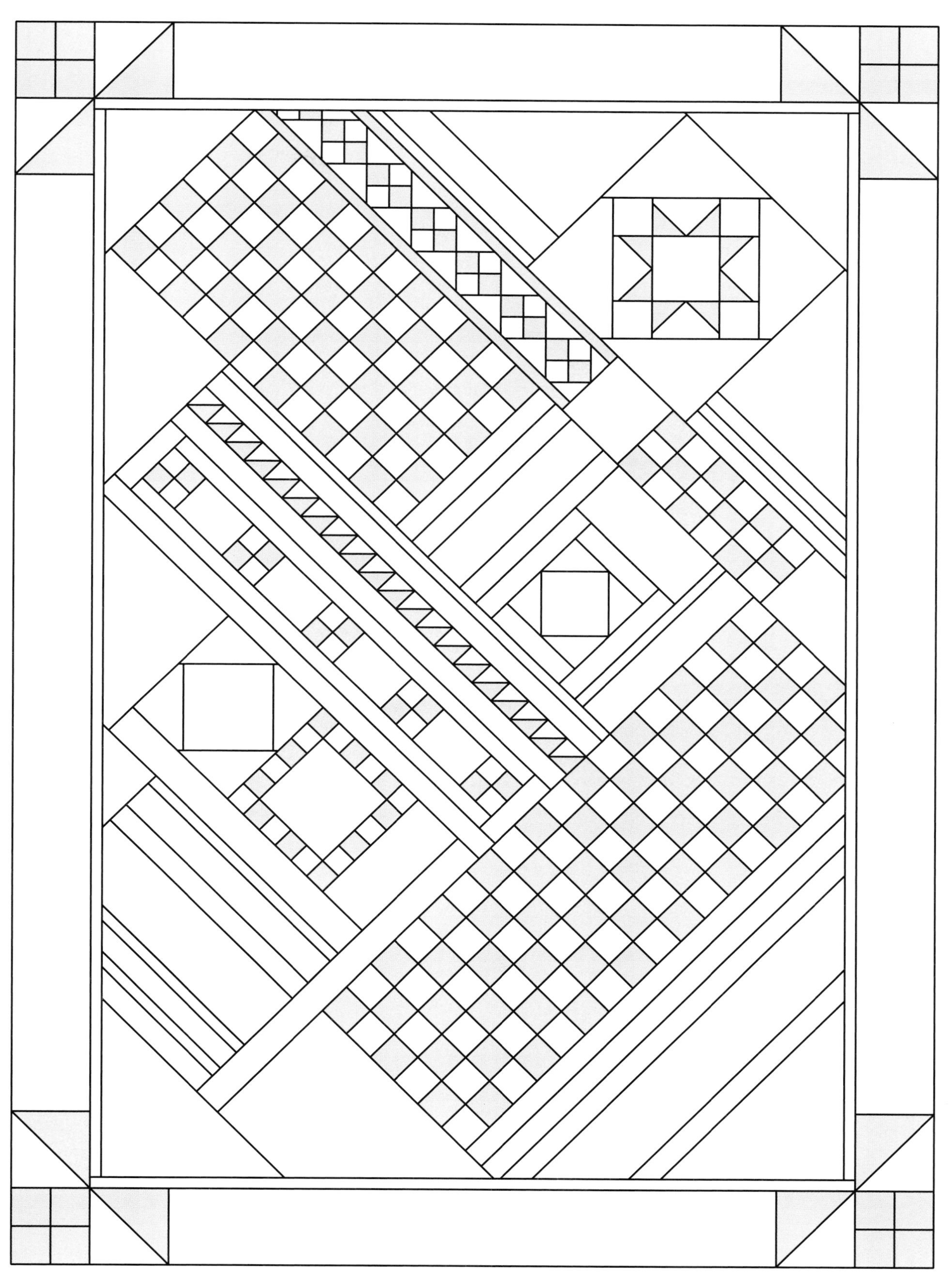

Block Placement diagram for
Let It Snow

African Rhythm

42" x 31", pieced and quilted by Linda K. Johnson

When we think of Africa, we think of the fabulous animals and beautiful people. We also picture an abundance of sunshine and bright colors. This was captured in African Rhythm with quite a variety of fabrics including cotton prints, batiks, and solids. Note how the earthy browns recede to let the motifs pop.

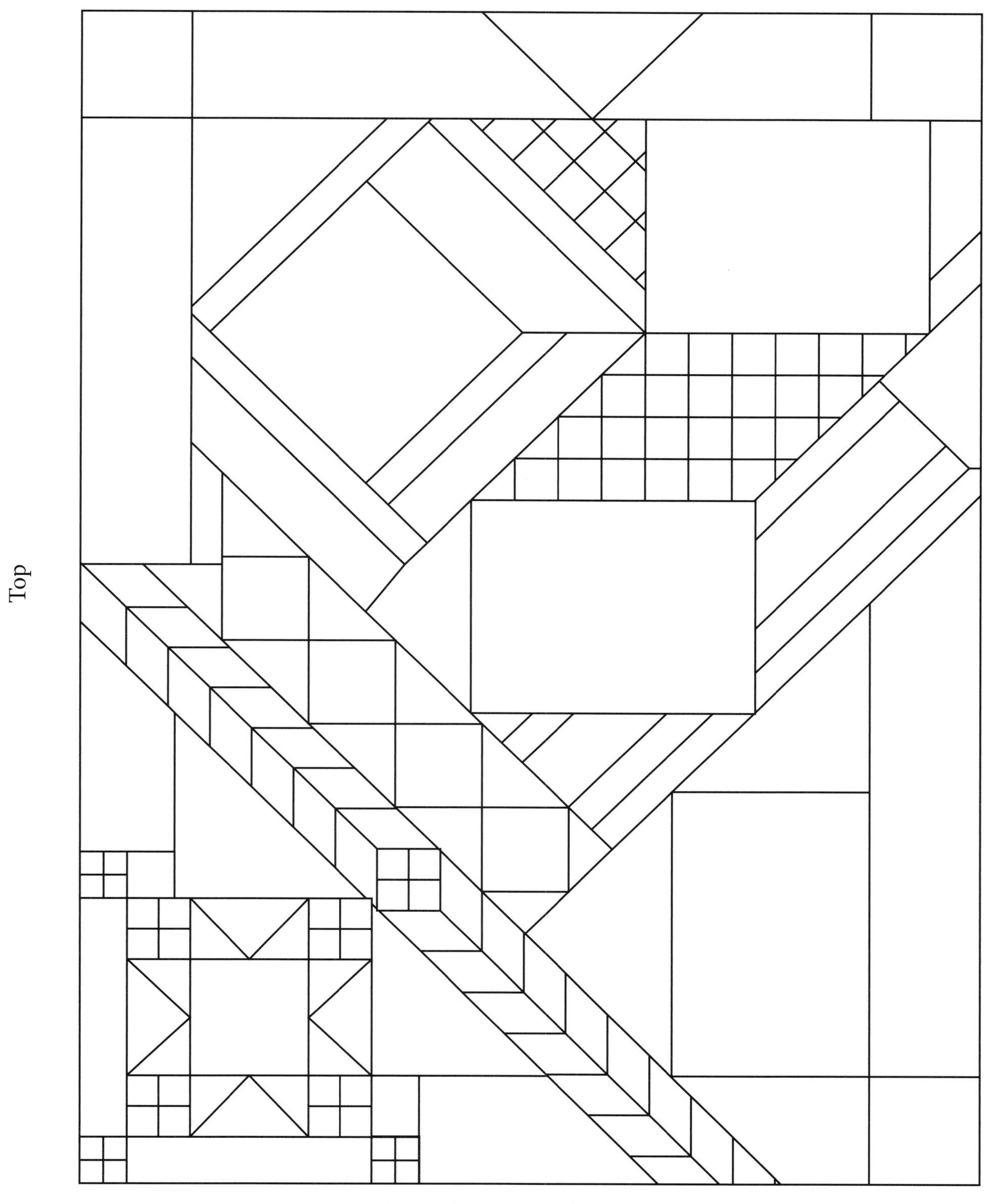

Block Placement diagram for
African Rhythm

African Safari

32" x 46", pieced and quilted by Jane K. Wells

Jane and her husband have been fortunate to enjoy several unbelievably awesome African safaris. When Jane was in the Gnoren Gnora Crater, she thought that this must be what heaven was like.

The large animal prints were chosen for their artistry. The batik woman and giraffe were bought in Africa as part of a large panel.

This quilt gives a feeling of the safari with the animals taking center stage surrounded by nature's greens and browns. Jane tried several browns before deciding that this mottled brown that glowed was just right.

African Safari is a variation of Big, Bold, and Beautiful. Although the same block placement diagram was used for both, you can see here that Jane made some changes. For example, she replaced the four Snowball blocks with an eight-pointed star with a fussy-cut center.

At the Zoo

32" x 44", pieced and quilted by Jane K. Wells

AT THE ZOO is a variation of UNDER THE SEA. Although the same block placement diagram was used for both, you can see here that Jane made some changes. For example, the four-patches in the Cross unit near the lower right corner were replaced with fussy-cut squares and the pieced unit below it was replaced with a strip-set.

That's So Kyla

48½" x 59", pieced and quilted by Jane K. Wells

When Jane's 16-year-old daughter, Kyla, was asked if she would like this style of quilt, she immediately said, "Oh, yeah...I want skulls and Hello Kitty in black, white, and hot pink." That's So Kyla is a very busy quilt using a great variety of fabrics. The border fabric is used liberally in the blocks, which gives a sense of unity to the quilt. Working within the parameters of Kyla's color scheme meant that her colors were the main colors, but bits of other bright colors were added for interest and excitement.

We're betting you can do this one without any block placement diagram at all!

Asian Influence by Sandi Brothers, Spencerville, Indiana
Variation of Big, Bold, and Beautiful

Big, Bold, and Beautiful by Sue Hobeck, Hicksville, Ohio
Variation of Big, Bold, and Beautiful

Moon Rabbits by Lynne Bogardus, Columbia City, Indiana
Quilted by Paula Reuille, Columbia City, Indiana
Variation of Guatemala en Rojo

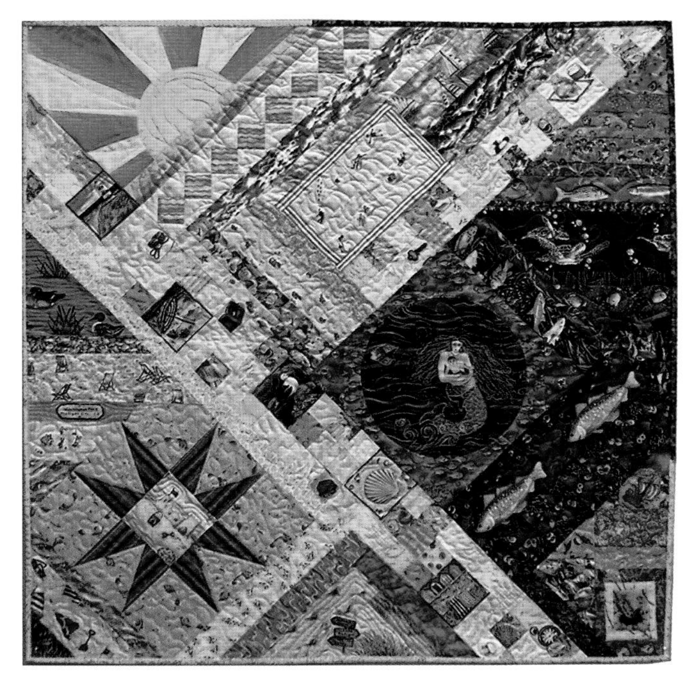

Lake Effect by Jan Lawhorn, Fort Wayne, Indiana
Variation of Christmas

Bodacious Roosters by Jane K. Wells, Fort Wayne, Indiana

Variation of Ah, Autumn!

Here A Pup by Judy Davis, Fort Wayne, Indiana

Variation of Here A Chick

Deloris Zonakis, Fort Wayne, Indiana

Variation of Let It Snow

Hooray for America by Georgetta Simmons

Fort Wayne, Indiana

Variation of That's So Kyla

Happy 50th Anniversary Tom and Doris by Jane K. Wells
Fort Wayne, Indiana
Variation of Here A Chick

You've Left Footprints in My Hert
by Vicki Slosson, Fort Wayne, Indiana
Variation of African Rhythm

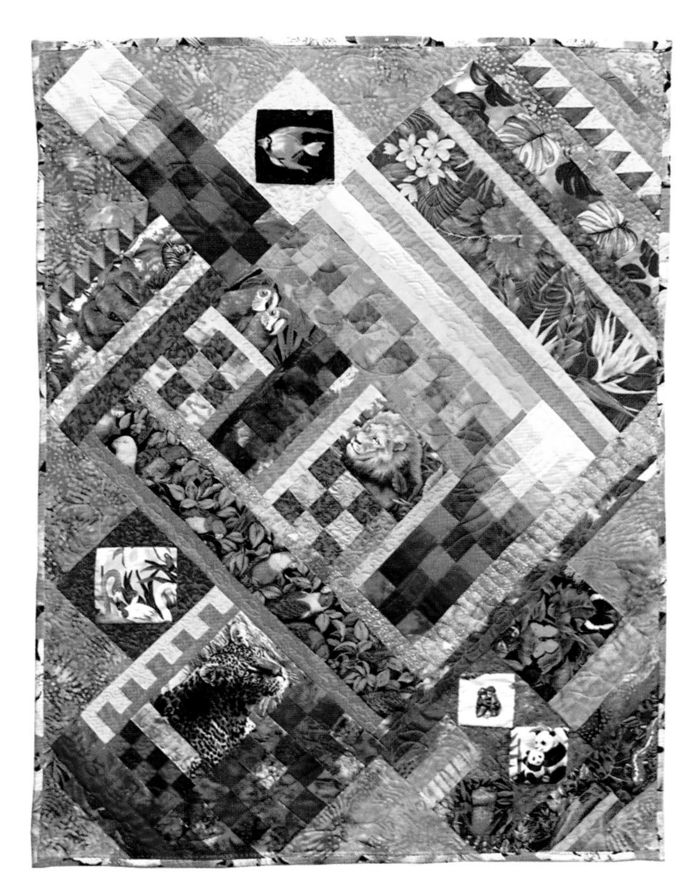

It's Been Wild by Deb Roehm, Roanoke, Indiana
Quilted by Paula Reuille, Columbia City, Indiana
Variation of Under the Sea

Every Quilt Needs a Little Chocolate by Cheryl Templeton
Fort Wayne, Indiana
Variation of Summer

TECHNIQUES

Bias Vines

Cut bias strips the size indicated in your pattern. Fold in half lengthwise, wrong sides together, and press.

For a ¼" vine, sew a generous ¼" seam from the folded edge. (For a ⅜" vine, use a generous ⅜" seam.)

Insert a ¼" or ⅜" bias bar, slide the seam allowance to the back, and press. Trim the seam allowance if necessary to keep it from showing on the front.

Baste vines in place, using an iron to gently shape them. Blind hem stitch the folded edges to the background with invisible or matching thread.

Borders

Measure the length of your quilt top through the middle of the quilt. Cut 2 strips of border fabric to that measurement, using the width specified in your pattern.

Sew to the sides of the quilt and press the seam allowance towards the border.

Measure the width of your quilt top across the middle, including the side borders. Cut 2 strips to that measurement, using the width specific in your pattern.

Sew to the top and bottom and press the seam allowance toward the border.

Broken Dishes

Make half-square triangles (page 79) from strips or squares as specified in your pattern. You need the same number of half-square triangles as the number of Broken Dishes units you want to make.

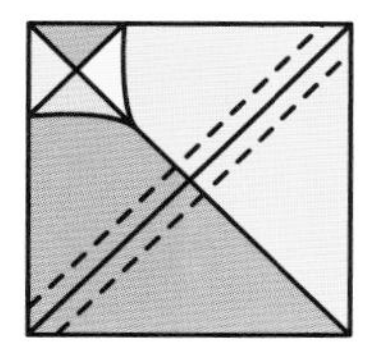

Draw a diagonal line on the back of a half-square triangle. Place right sides together with another half-square triangle, matching the seams but with the light and dark fabrics opposite each other. Sew ¼" on both sides of the diagonal line.

Cut on the diagonal line and press open. Trim to size.

Arrange Broken Dishes units in a strip, alternating the position of the fabrics as shown.

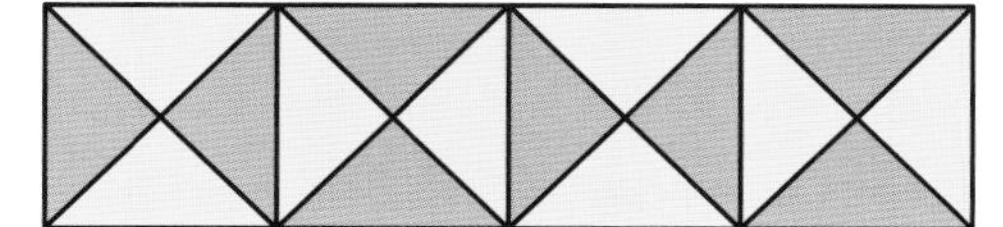

Checkerboard

Cut fabric strips as specified in your pattern.

Make a strip-set and press the seam allowance toward the darker fabric. Cut into segments as wide as the cut width of the strips.

Turn every other segment and sew together as shown.

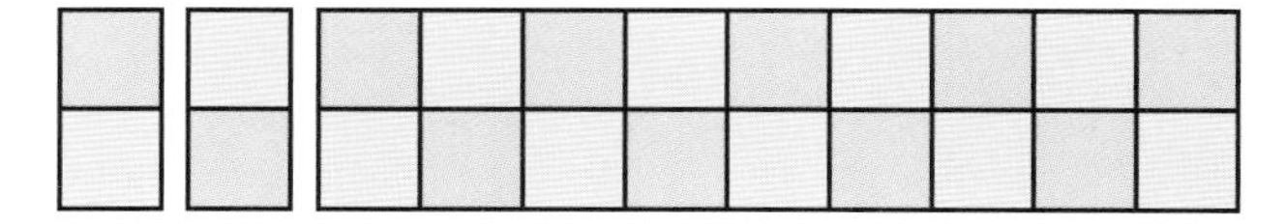

Alternatively, sew the units end-to-end

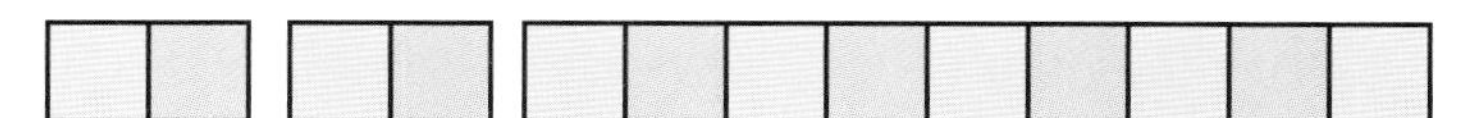

Chevron

Cut fabric strips as specified in your pattern. Sew half the strips together, offsetting them to the left by the finished width of the strips (or ½" less than the cut width of the strip). Sew the remaining strips together, offsetting them to the right as shown. Press the seam allowances in the two units in opposite directions.

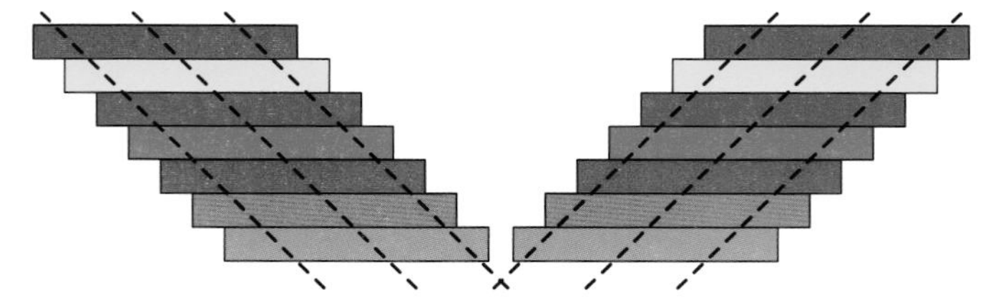

Place a long ruler at a 45-degree angle along one side of each strip-set and trim. Cut segments from each strip-set the width specified by your pattern.

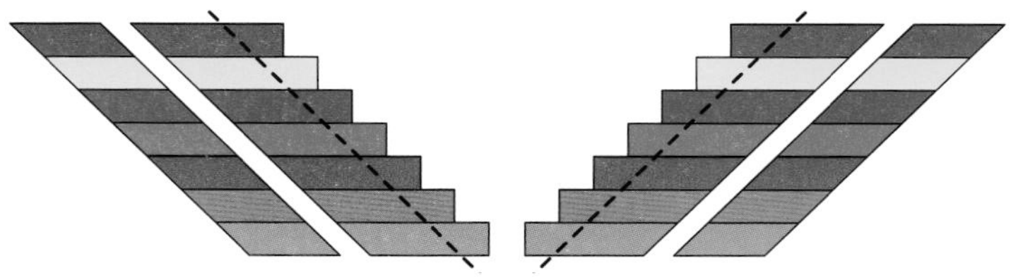

Sew pairs of segments from each strip-set together, nesting the seams allowances.

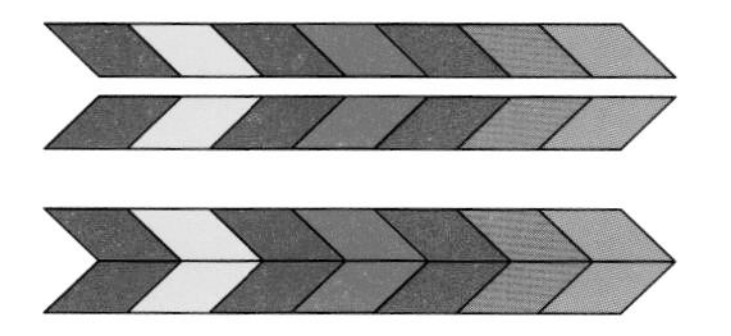

Circle in a Square

Instructions are given for a 12" finished block.

Cut a 12" square of focus fabric, centering the fabric's design as desired. Press with spray starch.

Cut a 13" square of background fabric.

Draw a 10" circle in the middle of a 12" square of freezer paper. Cut smoothly on your drawn line and discard the center circle.

Iron the shiny side of the paper onto the wrong side of the background square. Draw a pencil or chalk line on the fabric along the freezer-paper circle edge.

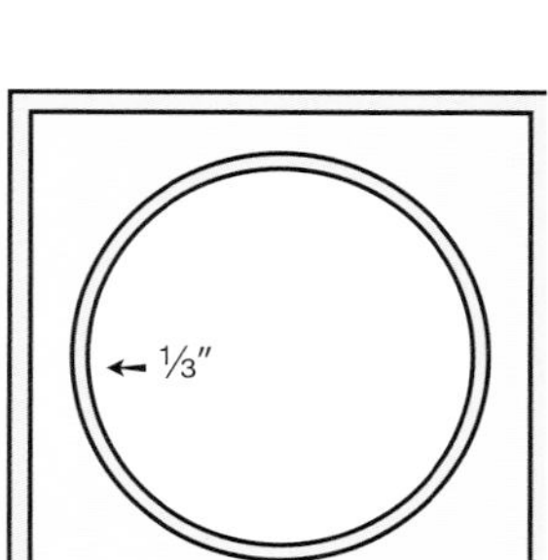

Cut out the center of the background fabric, leaving a 1⁄3" seam allowance along the edge of the freezer-paper template.

Keep

Discard

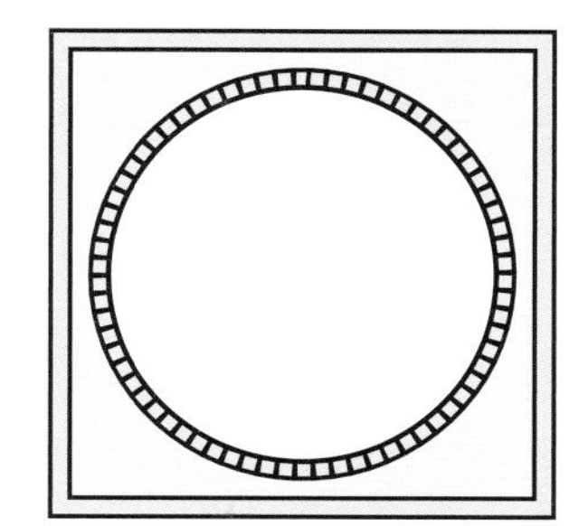

Clip the seam allowance almost to the freezer paper, every ½", leaving at least four threads of background seam allowance fabric intact.

Spray starch the seam allowance (or dab on starch) and press the clipped seam allowance back onto the freezer paper, keeping a smooth, even edge.

Apply a water-soluble glue stick on top of the seam allowance, but avoid getting glue on the freezer paper.

Place the background fabric on top of the focus fabric (right sides of both fabrics should be in view) and press with a hot iron so the two adhere to each other. Set aside to cool and let the glue set.

Gently lift the background fabric edges and remove the freezer paper.

Turn the circle and background fabric right side up, then lift one section of the background fabric up revealing the glued seam allowance. You will be able to see the circle you drew earlier.

Use your open toe foot or zipper foot to stitch exactly on your drawn line. Stitch all the way around the circle, pivoting as necessary with the needle down to get a precise, smooth circle.

Trim the seam allowance and excess focus fabric ¼" from your stitching line. Press and square the block to a 12½" square.

Fillers

Filler strips can be of one fabric or pieced of several fabrics to achieve the size you need. Larger areas can be filled with shapes cut from strip-sets, single fabrics, or a combination of both.

If a component doesn't quite fit, trim it off if it's too big or add a filler if it's too small.

Consider using leftover strips or partially pieced components, blocks, or appliqué from previous projects as fillers or even as your focus blocks.

The fun of this method is that you can do anything you want!

Flower Basket

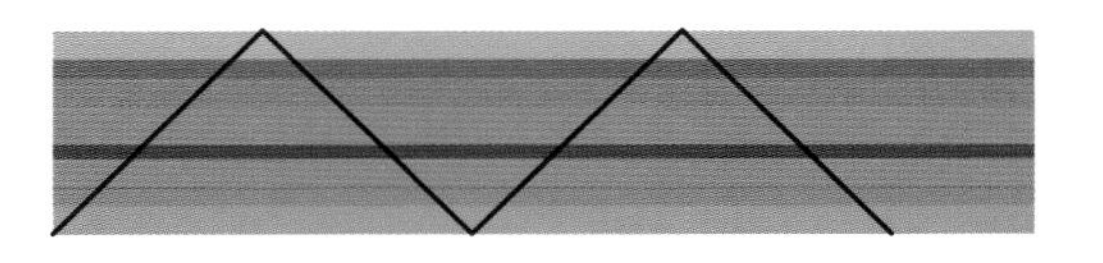

Cut two right-angled triangles from a striped fabric, placing the diagonal of a 6" ruler on the same stripe.

Stitch the right side of one triangle to the left side of the second triangle, matching the stripes, to form the basket base.

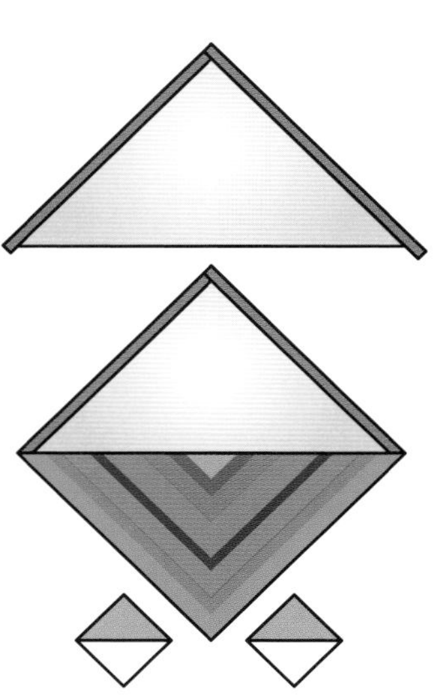

Cut a right-angled triangle with two 7½" legs from flower fabric. Add a 1" border to the sides for a basket handle. Trim the handle unit to the same size as the base. Stitch the base and handle units together. (Half-square triangles will be added during quilt construction to complete the base.)

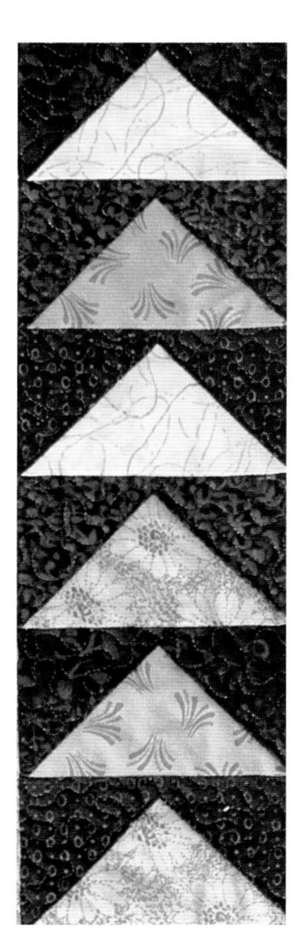

Flying Geese

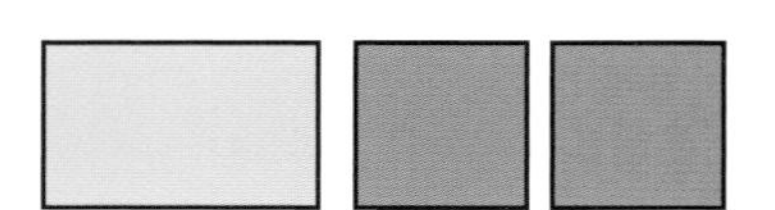

Cut the number of rectangles as specified in your pattern. Cut 2 squares of background fabric for each of the rectangles.

Draw a diagonal line on the back of the squares. Align a square with the end of a rectangle, right sides together. Stitch on the drawn line, as shown.

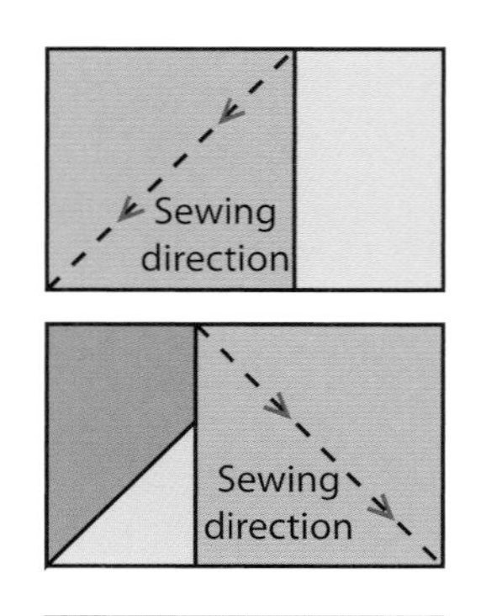

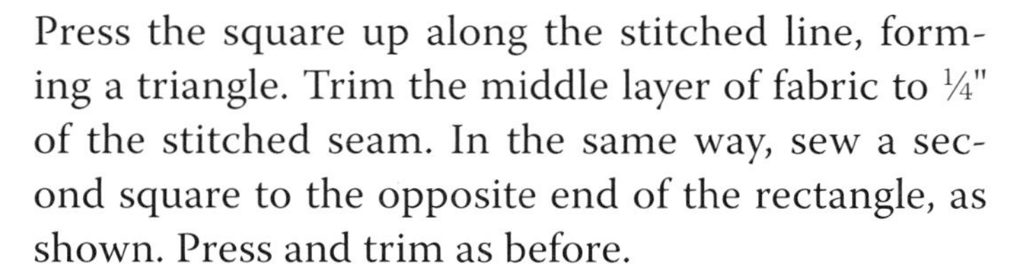

Press the square up along the stitched line, forming a triangle. Trim the middle layer of fabric to ¼" of the stitched seam. In the same way, sew a second square to the opposite end of the rectangle, as shown. Press and trim as before.

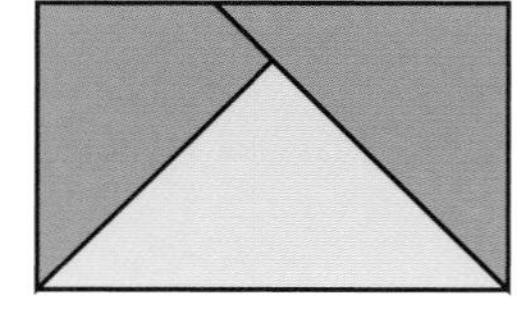

Four-Patch

Cut fabric strips as specified in your pattern.

Make a strip-set with 2 strips of contrasting fabrics and press the seam allowance toward the darker fabric. Cut into segments the same width as the width of the cut strips.

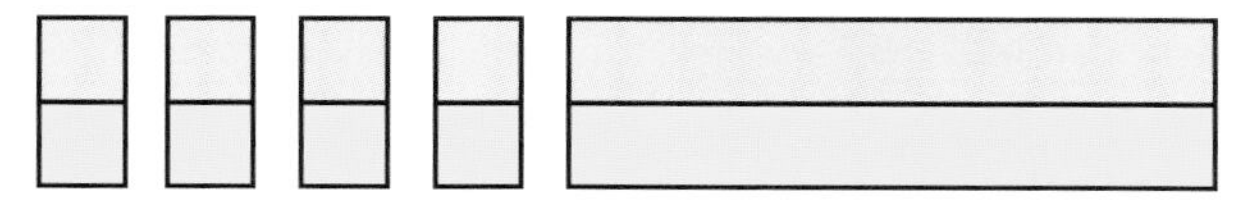

Turn 1 segment and sew 2 segments together as shown, nesting the seam allowances, to form a Four-Patch unit.

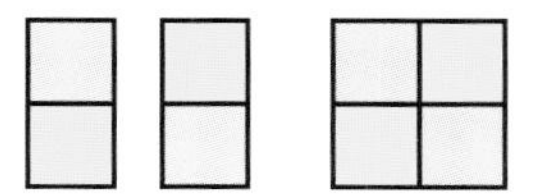

Friendship Star

Cut 4 background squares and 1 star center square from contrasting fabrics. Cut 2 more squares of each fabric ⅞" larger.

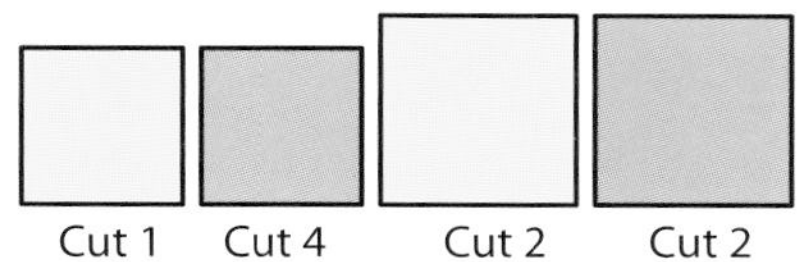

Make 4 half-square triangles using the larger squares, following the instructions for Half-Square Triangles from Squares (page 79).

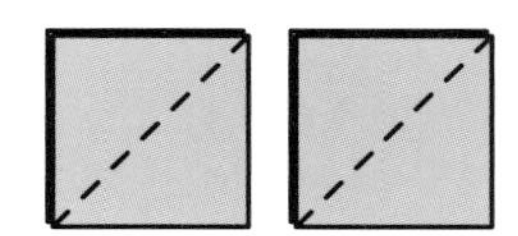

Arrange the units as shown. Sew into three rows, pressing the seam allowances in rows 1 and 3 toward the outer edges and the seam allowances in the middle row toward the center. Join the rows, nesting the seam allowances, to complete the star.

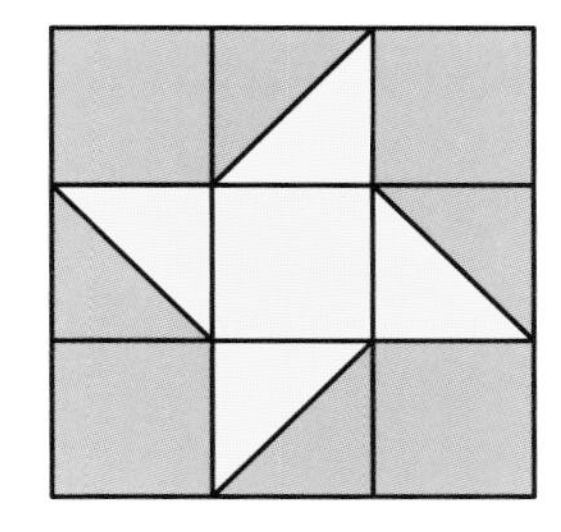

Fused Appliqué

Trace a master-appliqué pattern onto tracing paper. Use the back of the master pattern to trace and number the appliqué pattern pieces onto the paper side of fusible web about ½" apart.

Cut out the patterns about ¼" beyond the drawn lines.

Press the appliqué fabrics with spray starch to stabilize. Press the fusible-web pattern pieces onto the back side of the appliqué fabrics according to the manufacturer's directions. Cut out fused appliqué pieces on the drawn lines.

Construct multi-piece flowers on a Teflon® pressing sheet, placing pieces over or under other pieces as indicated by the dotted lines on the patterns.

Center the master pattern over the background fabric and position the appliqué pieces under the pattern.

Remove the master pattern and fuse the pieces in place. Edge stitch with a zigzag or blanket stitch.

Fussy Cuts

When cutting focus fabric squares, the centers for square-in-a-square units, or other shapes, ignore the grainline and pay attention to the fabric motifs instead. Center the motifs in the shape you are cutting.

Half-Square Triangles from Squares

Cut 2 squares of contrasting fabrics ⅞" larger than the finished size you need. For example, 2⅞" squares will make 2½" half-square triangles that finish to 2".

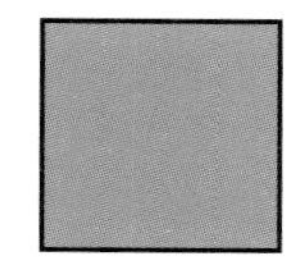

Draw a diagonal line on the back of the lighter square. Place the two squares right sides together, and sew ¼" on both sides of the drawn line. Cut along the drawn line. Open and press the seam allowance toward the darker fabric.

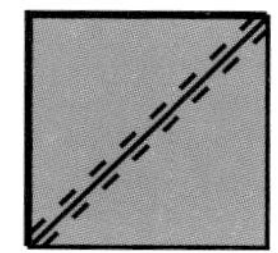
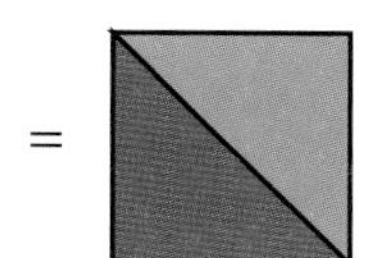
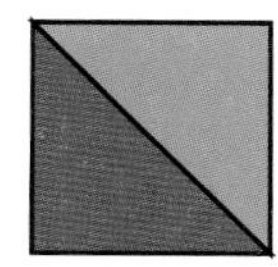

Half-Square Triangles from Strips

Cut 2 strips of contrasting fabrics.

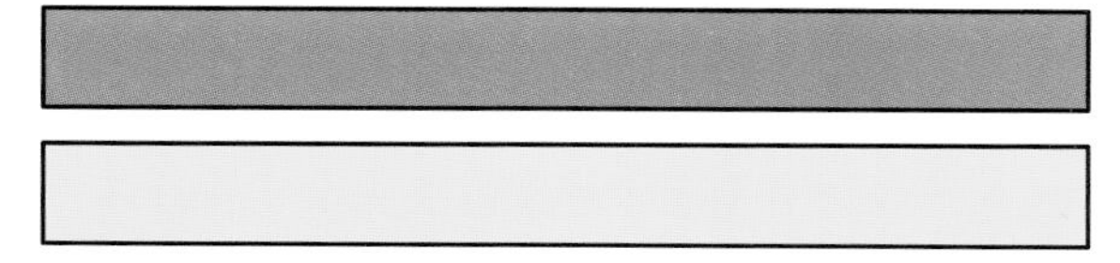

Draw parallel lines on the wrong side of the light fabric the same distance apart as the width of the strips. Then draw diagonal lines as shown.

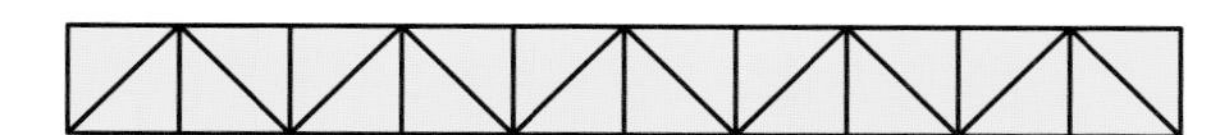

Place the strips right sides together and stitch ¼" on either side of the diagonal lines as indicated by the dashed lines. Cut apart on the solid lines. Open and press the seam allowance toward the darker fabric.

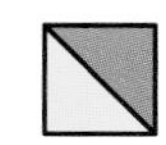
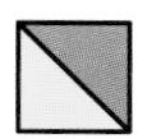

Trim to the unfinished size.

Lightning Bolt

Cut the number of rectangles specified in your pattern from each of two contrasting fabrics. Cut each rectangle on the diagonal as shown.

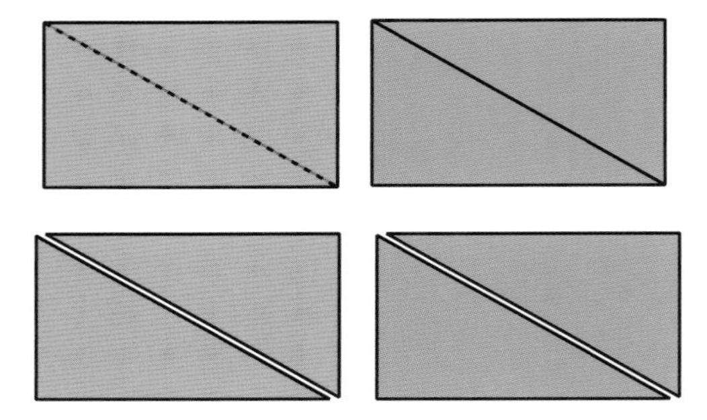

Note: Make sure you always cut the diagonal from the same two corners. If cutting two different fabrics at once, both should be right sides up

Place two triangles right sides together, with ½" tip of each triangle sticking out on each end (measure along the diagonal cut). Sew with a ¼" seam. Press the seam allowance toward the darker fabric and trim the tips.

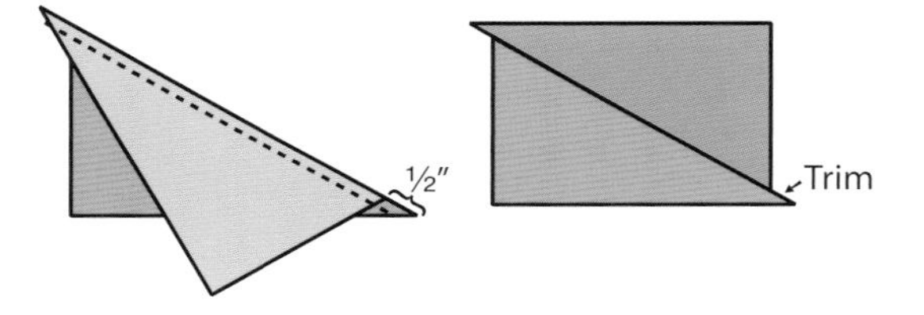

Note: The diagonal seam is ⅛" away from both corners. That is necessary for joining the rectangles together and having the diagonal finish in the corners, making perfect points.

Sew the specified number of rectangles together in a row. Make two rows. Add fillers at the end if indicated in your pattern. Offset the rows and sew them together.

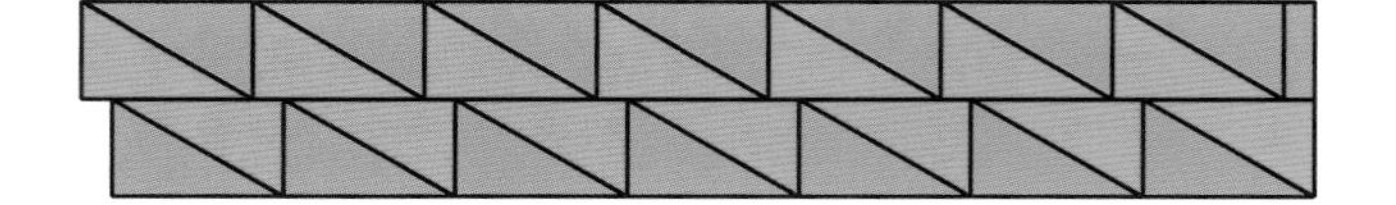

Log Cabin

Cut the center square or rectangle and strips for the logs according to your pattern instructions.

> *Note: Log widths can be all the same or random widths.*

Cut the first log to the size of the center square. Sew and press the seam allowance toward the log.

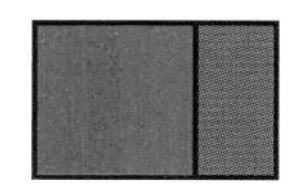

Cut the second log to the size of the center and first log. Sew and press as before.

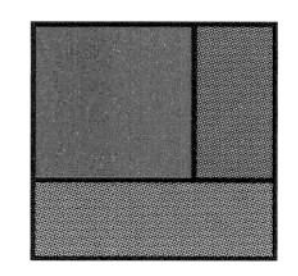

Cut the third log to the size of the center and second log. Sew and press.

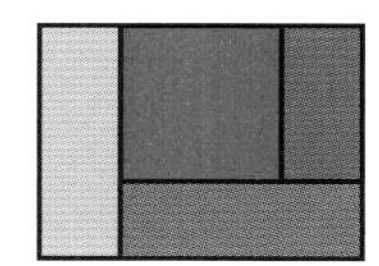

Cut the fourth log to the size of the center and two logs. Sew and press.

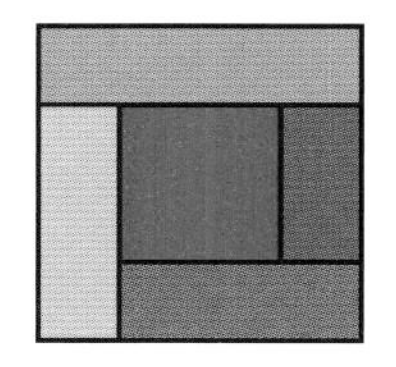

Continue in this manner until the block is as large as needed. Trim to size.

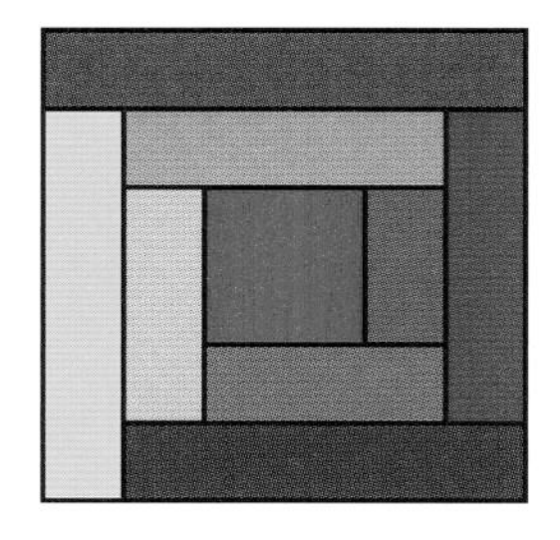

Variation: Add strips to just two adjacent sides of the "center" square for a half-Log Cabin block.

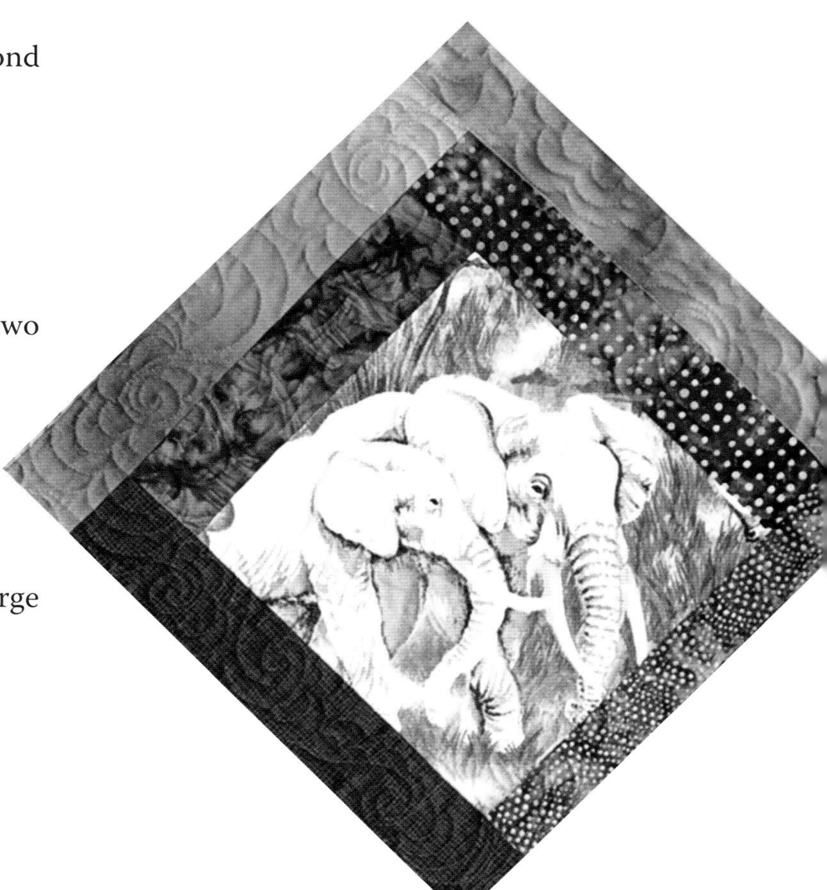

Mitered Border

To miter a border, sew the borders onto the sides of the quilt or block, stopping ¼" from the corner. Leave enough border fabric extending beyond the corner to accommodate the miter (width of border + 1").

From the front of the quilt, fold the top border back under itself at a 45-degree angle. Use a ruler with a 45-degree angle to check placement and make sure you have a square outer edge.

Press to form a crease in the folded border. Use blue painter's tape to hold the folded border in place from the front of the quilt, as shown.

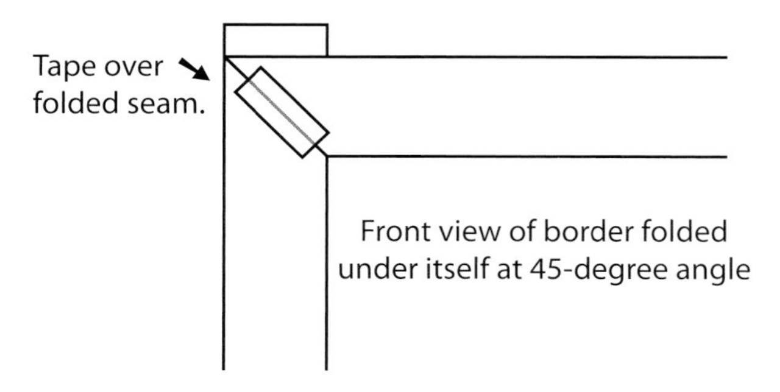

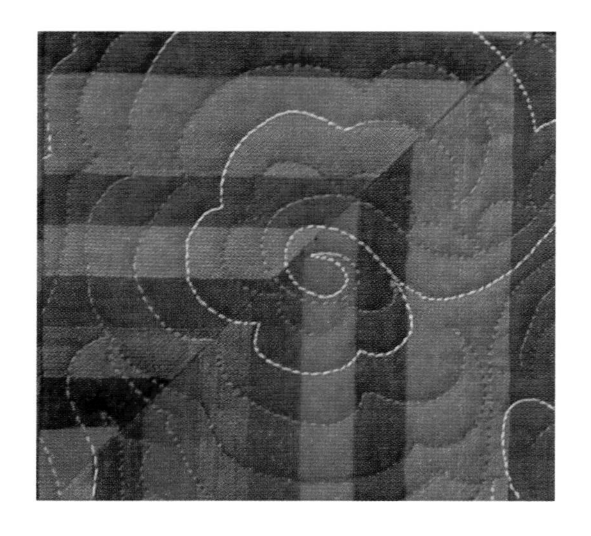

Fold the quilt and the taped border at a 45-degree angle, right sides together, with the outside edges of borders even with each other. Starting at the outside edge, sew along the fold, being careful not to catch the tape in the stitching. Stop ¼" from the quilt where the border seams meet.

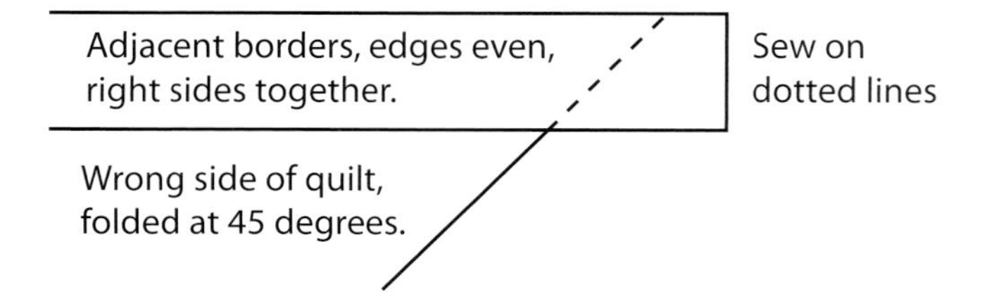

Remove the tape and trim the seam allowance to ¼". Gently press the seam open, being careful not to stretch the fabric.

Mitered Square

Use a striped fabric and, for ease of handling the bias edges, starch and press both sides before cutting, being careful to keep the stripes straight.

Use the size ruler for the square specified in your pattern (or tape off a larger ruler).
- 6½" square ruler for an 8½" square (8" finished)
- 6" square ruler for a 7" square (6½" finished)
- 4½" square ruler for a 5½" square (5" finished)

Align the center diagonal line on the ruler with a stripe on the fabric. Cut both sides of the triangle, then cut the base. Position the ruler on the same stripe for each triangle cut.

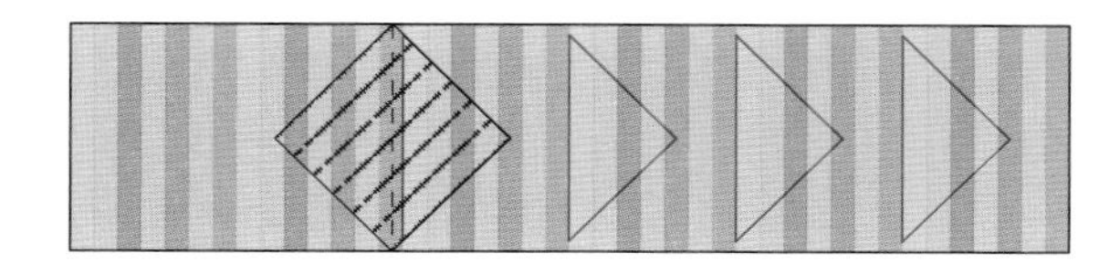

Sew the triangles together as shown to form a mitered square.

Mitered Square Triangles

Cut triangles as you would for a mitered square using the size ruler specified in your pattern. Sew to the sides of a square or block as directed in the square-in-a-square instructions on page 88.

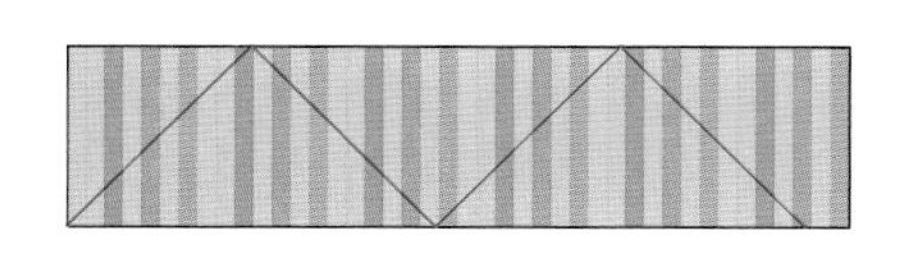

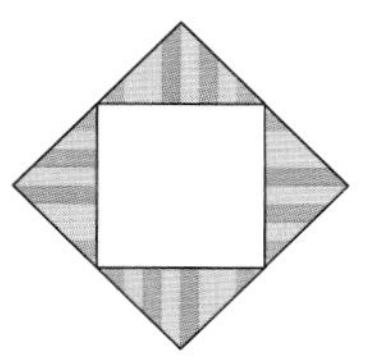

Tip: You could use a larger square ruler than specified and mark off the size square you need with masking tape.

Nine-Patch

Cut fabric strips of contrasting fabrics as specified in your pattern.

Make 2 strip-sets as shown and press the seam allowances toward the darker fabric. Cut into segments the same width as the width of the cut strips.

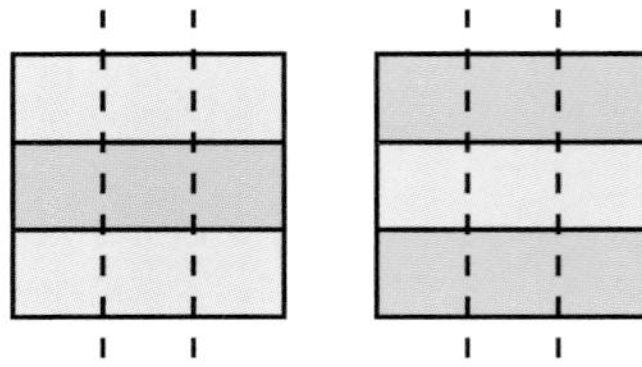

Sew 3 segments together as shown, nesting the seam allowances to form the Nine-Patch units.

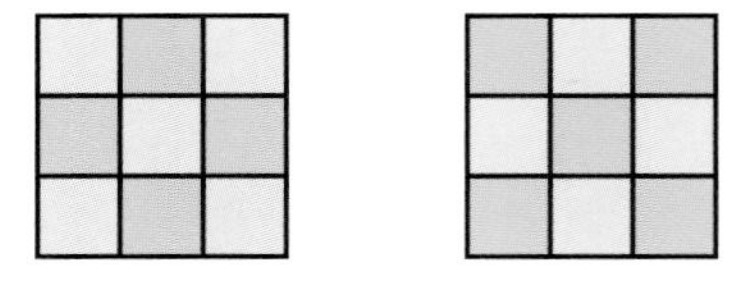

Paper Piecing

Enlarge the pattern if directed to do so.

Trace the paper piecing pattern onto thin paper, copying sequence numbers and registration marks.

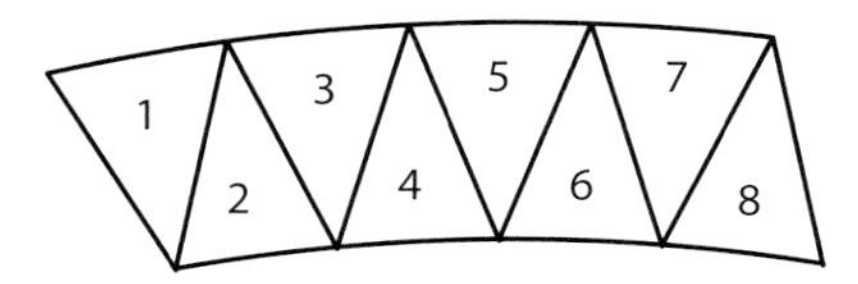

Cut each fabric at least 1" wider and longer than the widest and longest part of each paper-piecing section.

Place the first 2 fabrics, right-sides together, on the back of the foundation with the wrong side of the #1 fabric covering the #1 section and extending ¼" beyond the sewing line between #1 and #2. Sew exactly on the line between #1 and #2, extending the stitching about ¼" into the seam allowance.

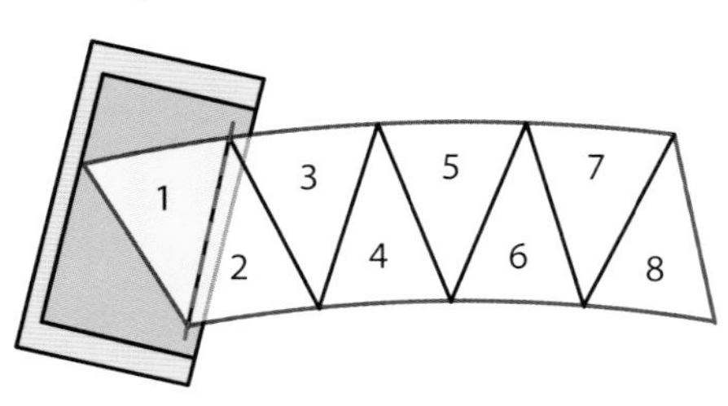

Flip the second fabric to cover the #2 section and press it flat. Fold the paper back along the sewing line between #2 and #3 and trim the fabric that covers the #2 area ¼" beyond the sewing line.

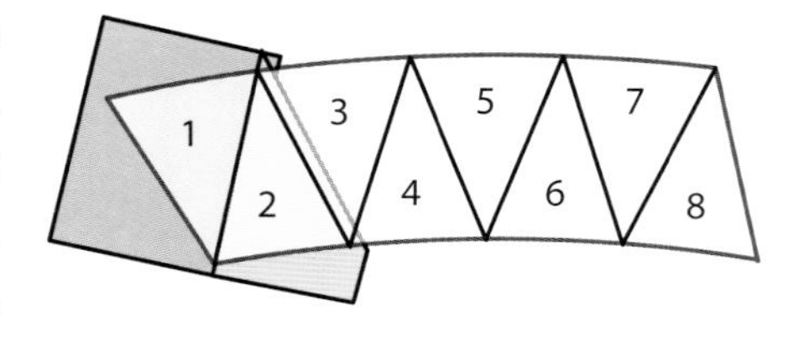

Align the edge of the #3 fabric with the trimmed seam allowance of #2, right sides together. Sew on the line between #2 and #3, flip fabric open and press flat. Fold the paper back along the sewing line between #3 and #4. Trim the seam allowance to ¼".

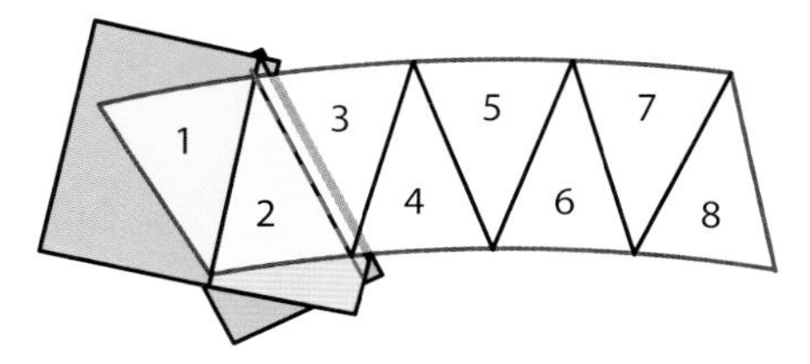

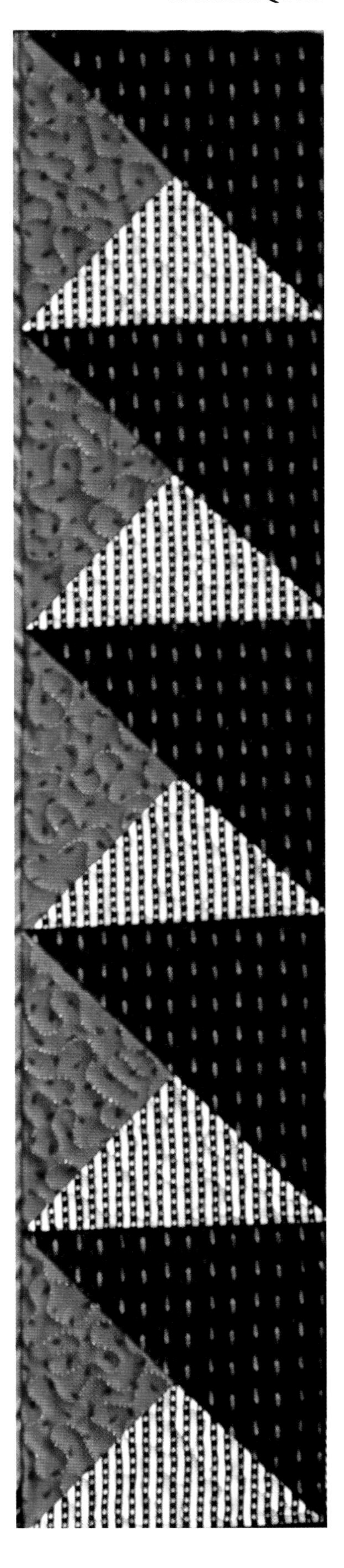

Continue in this manner until each piece is sewn on. Press, then trim on the cutting lines. Transfer any registration marks. Remove paper when directed by the pattern.

When joining curved units, clip the paper-pieced concave curve seam allowance, and pin to the convex curve unit, matching the ends and registration marks. Sew exactly on the seam line with the concave curve piece on top.

Ribbon

Cut squares as shown.

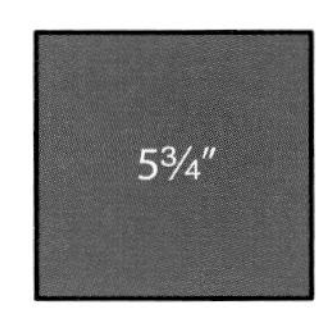

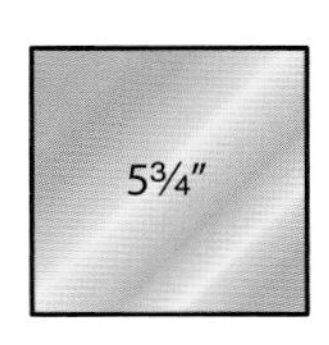

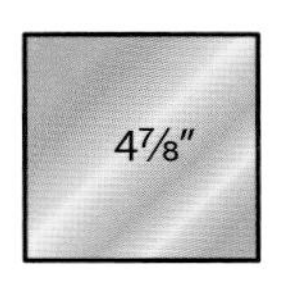

Make a half-square triangle with the larger squares following the instructions for Half-Square Triangles from Squares (page 79).

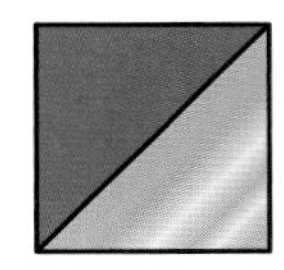

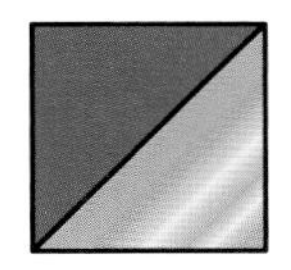

Draw a diagonal line on the back of the smaller square parallel to the stripes. Place right sides together with a half square triangle, with the drawn line the opposite direction of the half-square triangle seam. Sew ¼" on both sides of the drawn line. Open and press. Cut apart as shown.

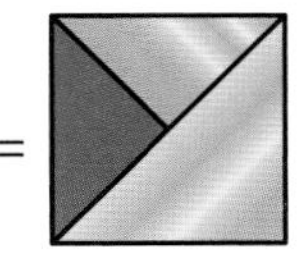

Arrange the units as shown in the figure OR use half the units to make a strip as shown in the photo.

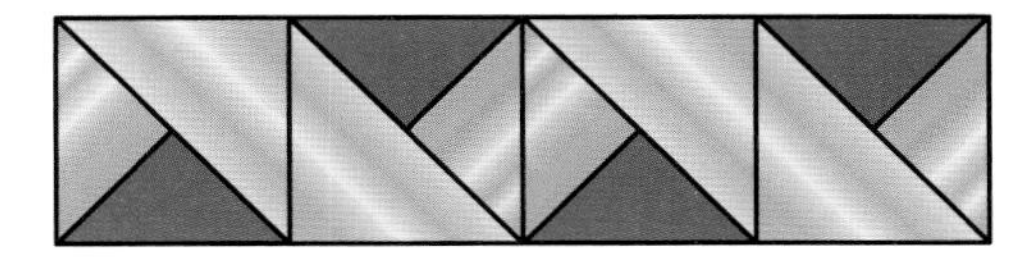

Rocking Squares

Cut a center rectangle or square of focus fabric as specified in your pattern. Cut a rectangle of border fabric at least 4"–5" wider and 3"–4" longer than the sides of the focus fabric block.

Cut the rectangle into wedges as shown.

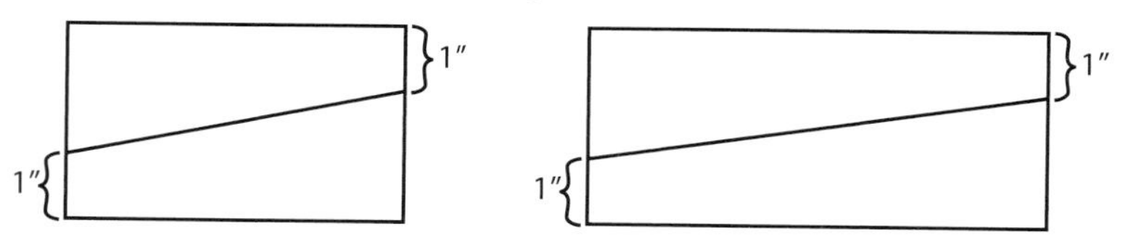

Sew the bias-cut side of the wedges to the top and bottom of the center square, positioning the narrow ends opposite each other as shown. Trim even with the center square.

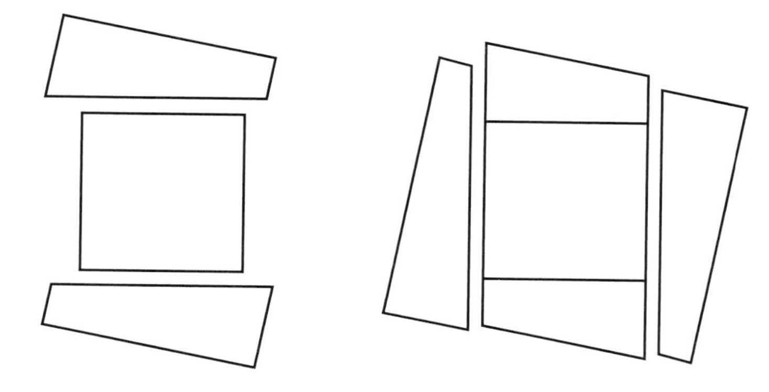

Cut a second rectangle 3"–4" longer than the center square plus the top and bottom border. Cut as before and add to the sides.

Trim with a square ruler, the size stated in the pattern.

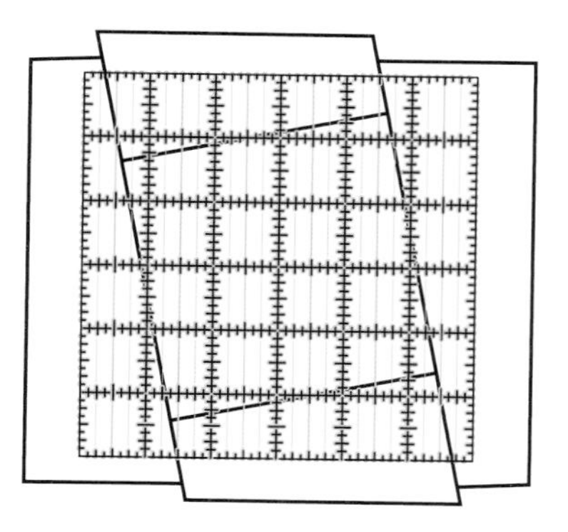

Setting Triangles

Cut a square the size indicated in your pattern.

For corner triangles with the straight-of-grain on the short sides, cut once on the diagonal.

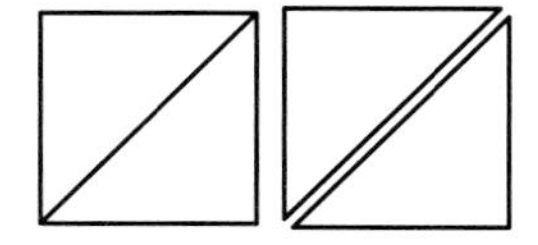

For side-setting triangles with the straight-of-grain on the long side (hypotenuse), cut twice on the diagonal.

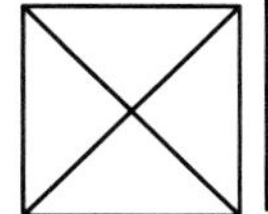
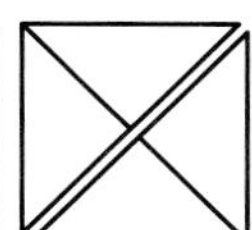
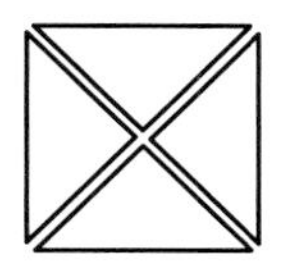

Snowball

Cut two sets of squares, the number and size specified in your pattern. Draw a diagonal line on the wrong side of the smaller squares.

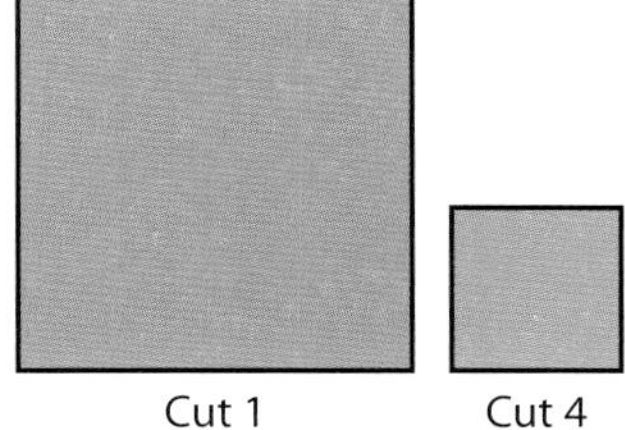

Sew 4 small squares to the corners of the larger square along the drawn lines. Trim the seam allowances of the smaller squares to ¼" and press the triangles towards the corners.

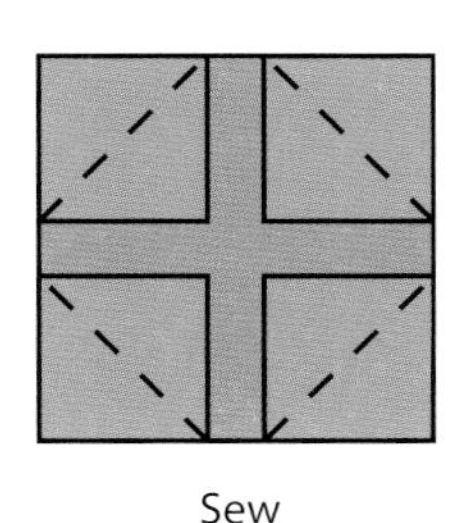
Sew

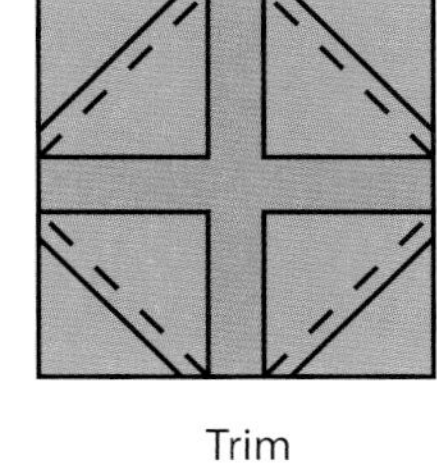
Trim

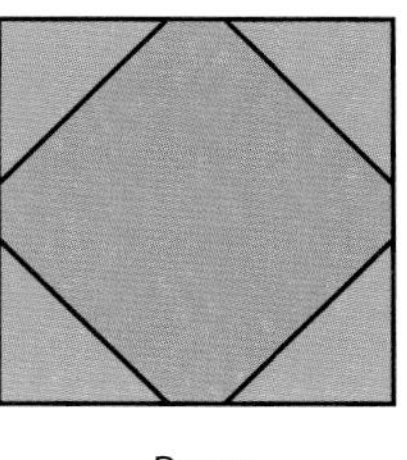

Press

Square-in-a-Square

Cut 1 square of focus fabric and 2 squares of background fabric for each square-in-a-square unit. Refer to your pattern for the sizes.

Cut the 2 squares of background fabric in half on the diagonal as shown.

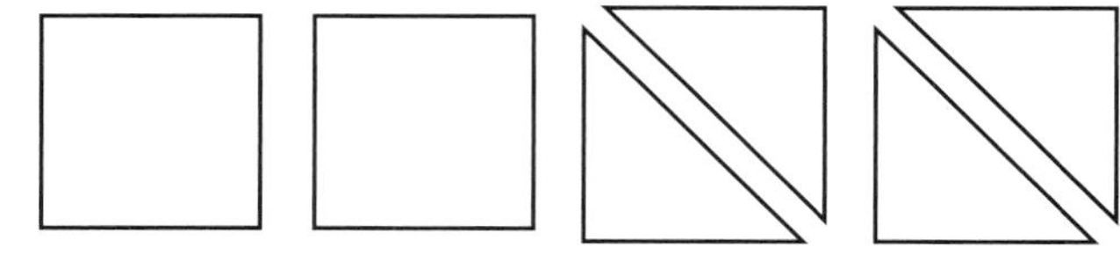

Center and sew 2 triangles to opposite sides of the focus fabric square. Press. Trim the points. Repeat. Trim to size.

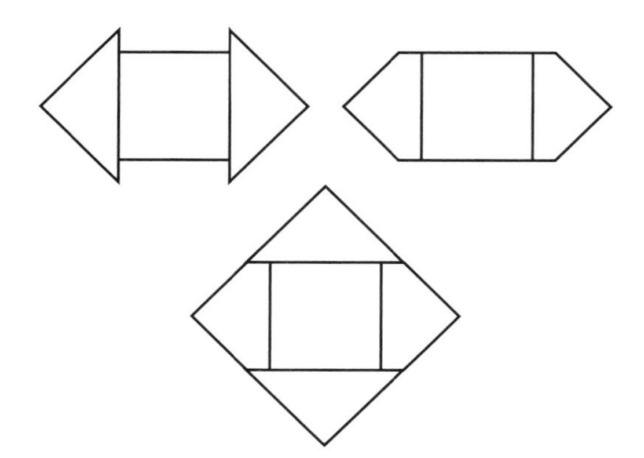

Squares-on-Point Strip

Cut one set of center squares and one set of outer squares as specified in your pattern. Cut the larger squares twice on the diagonal.

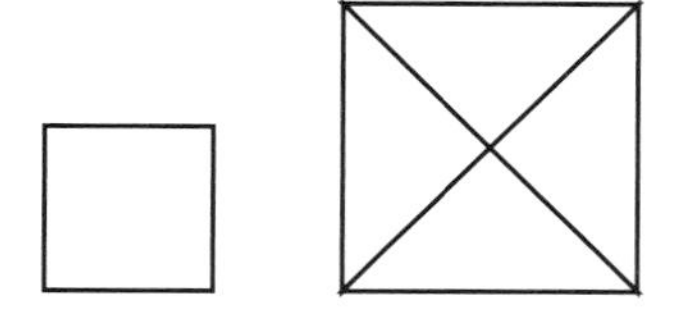

Sew a triangle to opposite sides of the each center square with the straight-of-grain to the outside, as shown. Trim the tips even with the center square. Press all the seam allowances toward the center square.

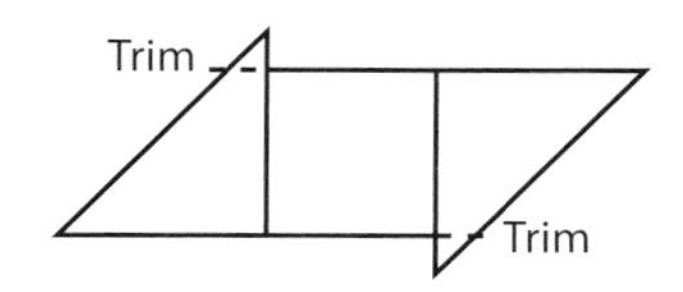

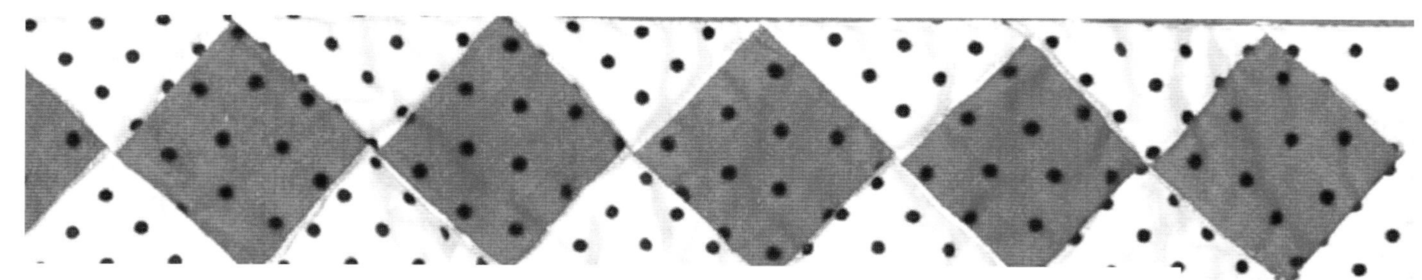

Sew the center-square units together, offsetting them on the diagonal as shown and nesting the seam allowances. Add an extra triangle at each end to complete the strip. Trim the sides ¼" from the points of the center squares or to the overall width of the squares-on-point strip as directed in your pattern.

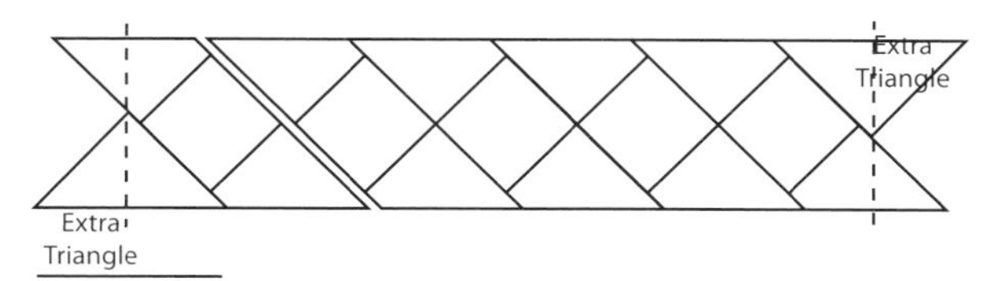

Squaring Up

Square up your quilt top as suggested in each pattern. Sometimes, each section is squared up as you progress, but other times it is advantageous to wait until all the sections are joined.

Start in a corner. Position a large square ruler (16"–22") so that the diagonal and the outside edges of the quilt are lined up with the ruler. Use a long (24") ruler as an extension by butting it up against the square ruler, as shown on page 8. Trim the edges even with the ruler with a rotary cutter.

Repeat at the other corners, repositioning the quilt as necessary, trimming the sides and corners as you move around the quilt. Trim as little as possible while ensuring that all the edges are straight and the corners square.

Star—Ohio or Eight-Pointed

Cut the center, background, and star-point pieces as instructed in your pattern. For example:

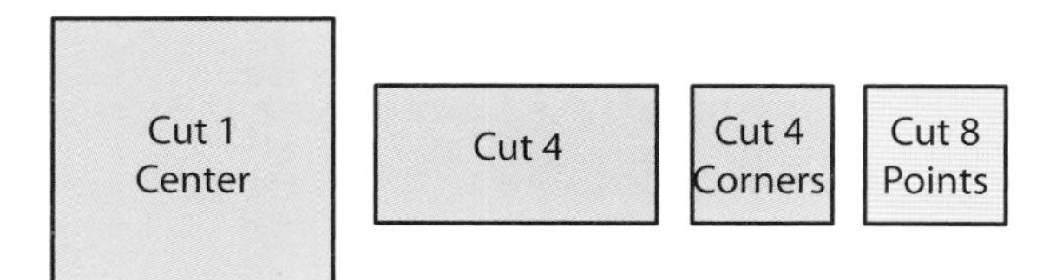

Make 4 star point units following the instructions for Flying Geese (page 76).

Arrange the pieces as shown.

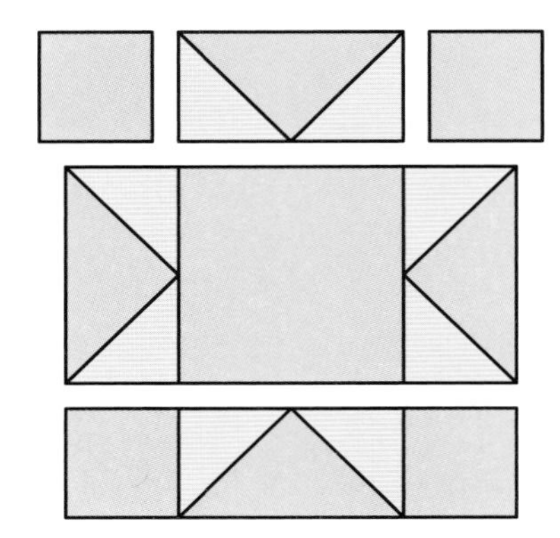

Sew into three rows, pressing the seam allowances in rows 1 and 3 out and the seam allowances in the middle row toward the center. Join the rows, nesting the seam allowances.

Star—Paper-Pieced Points

Trace 4 star point paper-piecing foundations onto tracing paper (page 84).

Cut background fabric squares and star point fabric according to the measurements in your pattern.

Place a background square right side out on back of a foundation and pin in place. Fold the foundation along the line between #1 and #2 and trim the excess to ¼". Repeat trimming on the other side.

Sew the star point pieces according to the instructions for paper-piecing (pages 84–85). Trim to the cutting line.

Arrange as shown. Sew into three rows, pressing the seam allowances in rows 1 and 3 out and the seam allowances in the middle row toward the center. Join the rows, nesting the seam allowances.

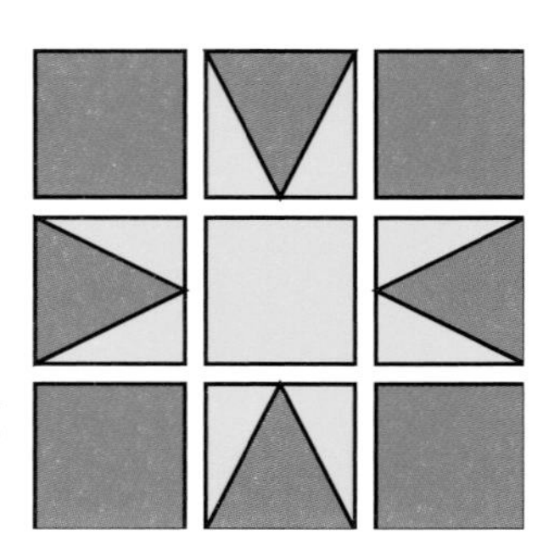

Remove the paper.

Star Strip

Cut the background, star center, and star point fabrics according to your pattern.

Make the star-point units in the same manner as Flying Geese (page 76) with the background squares and rectangles as shown.

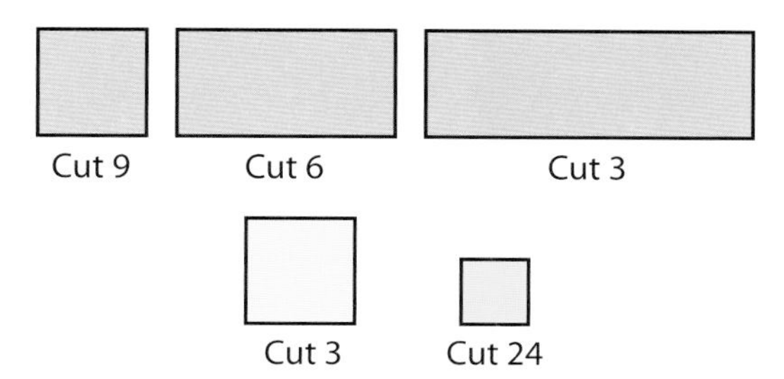

Arrange as shown. Sew into three rows, pressing the seam allowances in rows 1 and 3 out from the star centers and the seam allowances in the middle row toward the star centers. Join the rows, nesting the seam allowances.

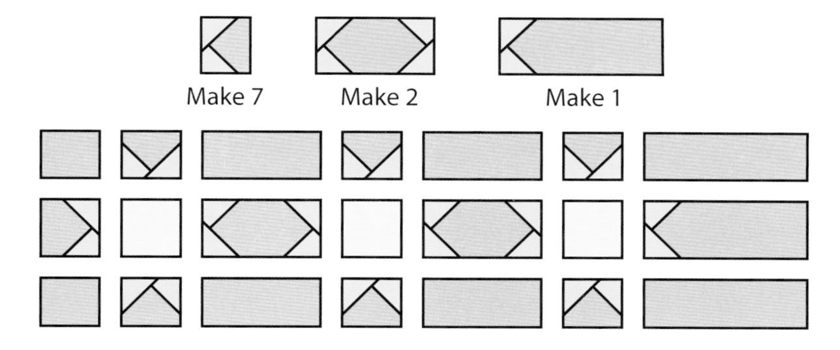

Strip Piecing

This is a great technique when a large filler is needed. It is important to use a variety of values, scales, and widths of strips. Follow your pattern for width of strips or make up your own, as long as your finished strip-pieced unit fits the pattern requirements.

Starting with either the widest or longest strip, place the next strip right sides together and stitch a ¼" seam.

Gradually sew on more fabric strips on both sides until you have the width called for in the pattern. Cut to the size and shape indicated.

Some patterns ask you to offset the strips as you add them to the set and then cut at a 45-degree angle. The offset should be equal to the width of the strip you're adding.

Press all the seam allowances in the same direction.

Yo-Yos

Cut out a circle of the diameter specified in your pattern.

Hand baste a ⅛" hem around the edge of the circle.

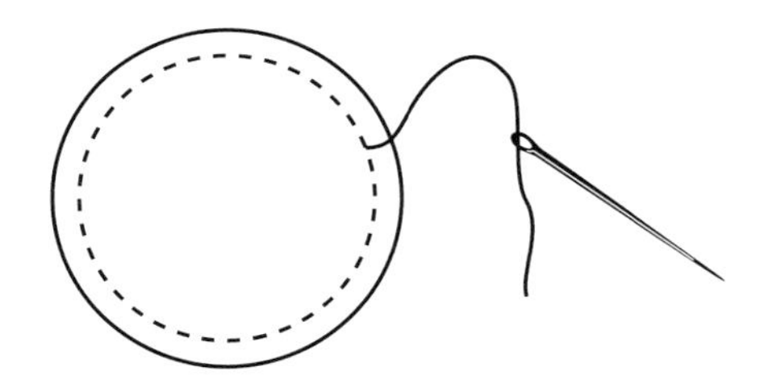

Pull the basting thread to gather the circle up and then secure the gathers with a few back-stitches.

Zipper

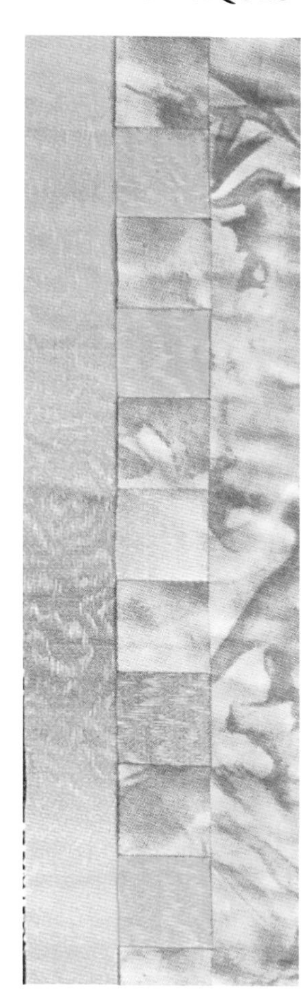

Cut 2 strips from contrasting fabrics into segments specified in your pattern.

Make an end-to-end checkerboard with the shorter segments. Sew the longer strips to the sides as shown.

Press the seam allowance toward the outer strips.

Resources

Haitian Embroidery

We used Haitian embroidered squares as the star centers in I GIVE YOU THE SUN, THE MOON AND THE STARS.

HAPI embroidered designs are created by the hands of women in the mountain village of Mizak, Haiti. This growing business is giving them an opportunity to work their way out of extreme poverty with dignity. Your purchase makes it possible for women to put food on the table and allows all their children an education. Their main product is a line of hand-embroidered framable greeting cards but you may also purchase unassembled hand-embroidered cloth for your quilt design. Visit them at www.HaitianArtisans.com to learn more about these talented women with Haitian Artisans for Peace International and to place orders.

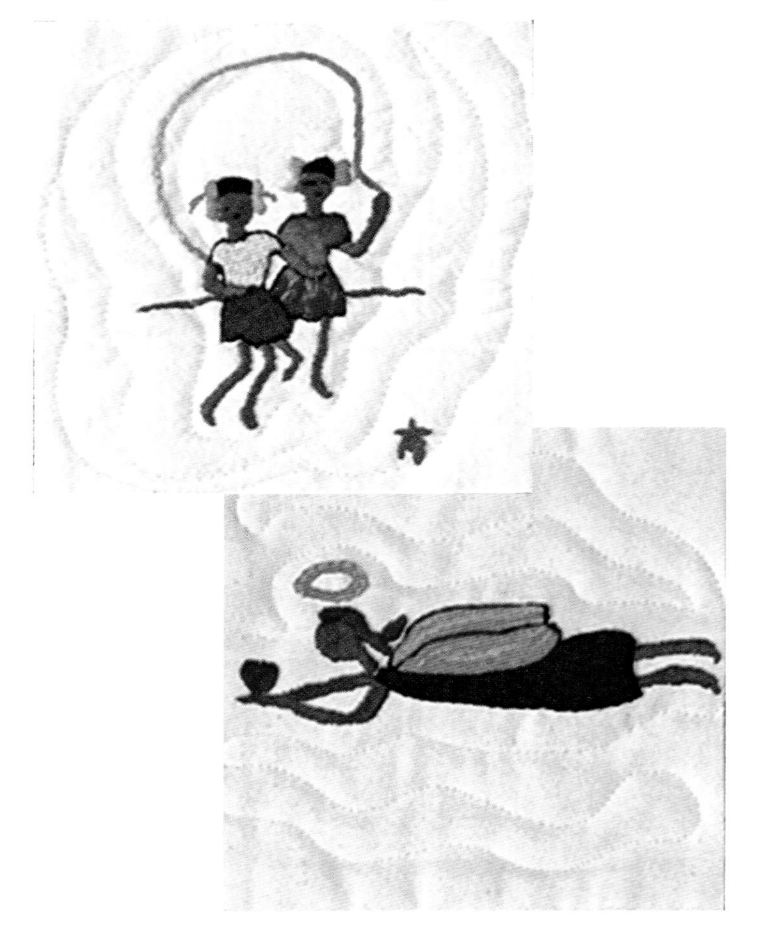

Guatemalan Fabric

During a wonderful vacation in Guatemala, Central America, we fell in love with the beautiful colors and texture of the hand-woven Guatemalan fabric. It was fascinating to watch the native Mayan people weave their magic on back-strap looms. We are so excited to be able to import this fabric from the Mayan weavers to share with quilt and fabric lovers in the United States.

This fabulous fabric is 100 percent cotton and machine washable and dryable. Guatemalan fabric has a looser weave, much like homespun fabric. It becomes soft after washing with a wonderful feel and texture.

We also have a selection of our original Crafty Ol' Broads patterns available online. We specialize in designing patterns that appear more complicated than they are to make. Send us an e-mail if your quilt guild or group is interested in having us come for a lecture or workshop.

Shop with us at www.craftyolbroads.com

Enjoy!

And Just Who Are Those Crafty Ol' Broads?

Sisters Linda K. Johnson (left) and Jane K. Wells (right) are award-winning quilters who love every aspect of quilting and just happen to be crafty, old, and broad!

In 2001, soon after we took our first quilt class, we started designing our own patterns, dreaming up new patterns while non-quilters were sleeping. We then started the Crafty Ol' Broads pattern and fabric company. We specialize in designing quilt patterns that appear much more complicated to make than they actually are. Our work is often inspired by the beauty of nature, art, and antique quilts.

In 2005, we began teaching and lecturing as a team. We are passionate about sharing our knowledge and love of quilting through our many classes and lectures where we introduce quilters of all levels to our unique patterns. We constantly challenge each other to create new techniques. Watch out because we are likely to "quilt talk" with anyone who is even remotely interested.

Our quilts have been selected for distinction in shows and contests both locally and nationally. Three of our quilts have appeared in two recent *New Quilts from an Old Favorite* books that document a yearly contest sponsored by the Museum of the American Quilter's Society. Our quilts have also been "the show" at various art galleries.

Other AQS Books

This is only a small selection of the books available from the American Quilter's Society. AQS books are known worldwide for timely topics, clear writing, beautiful color photos, and accurate illustrations and patterns. The following books are available from your local bookseller, quilt shop, or public library.

Look for these books nationally.
Call or **Visit** our Web site at

1-800-626-5420
www.AmericanQuilter.com